Sweetheart
Jewelry and Collectibles

Nicholas D. Snider

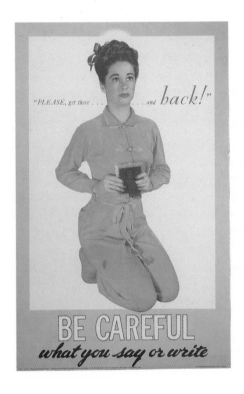

77 Lower Valley Road, Atglen, PA 19310

Published by Schiffer Publishing, Ltd.
77 Lower Valley Road
Atglen, PA 19310
Please write for a free catalog.
This book may be purchased from the publisher.
Please include $2.95 postage.
Try your bookstore first.

We are interested in hearing from authors
with book ideas on related subjects.

Title page:

Who is she and what is she thinking? A sweetheart prays for her loved one to return. The words that must have rushed through her mind: fear, loss, love, pain, and worry while praying to a higher power for strength.

So many women watched as their loved one went off to do their part. Women picked up the wrenches and turned on the switches to do their best to support their heroes who were in harm's way.

This picture should be a visible reflection of what war does when it comes between lovers. The old adage "one picture worth a thousand words" was never truer.

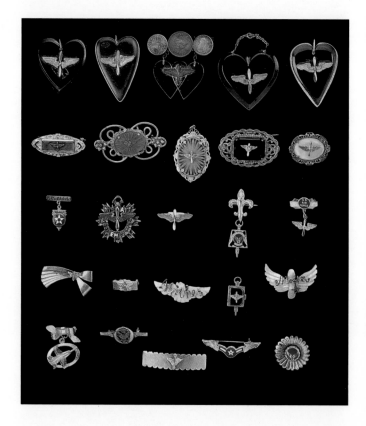

Jewelry from the early 1900s to the early 1960s. The Lucite hearts are hand made, 1940-1945 era. This is a good example of the glass, Lucite, mother-of-pearl and metals that offered a wide variety of items to be worn.

CONTENTS

ACKNOWLEDGEMENTS

Recognizing people for the contributions they have made to this book will cause joy for many and pain for a few. To those few who I have overlooked, please accept my apology and know that the omission of your name is not an intentional oversight. For lack of anything else, I will blame the power surges in my PC. You all have done much to make my collection one of the finest in the world. To you all, I say thank you.

Now, to those of you who I have listed; if you think for one minute you are the reason this book is so good, since you provided me material for my collection, you are right! You are very special people and I'd like to continue thinking you believed me when I said I wanted to protect a piece of American history by documenting items that relate to men and women in the Armed Forces. I have listed your names and where you were located when we transacted business. Hopefully you are still out there and will continue to make contributions to this wonderful area of collecting. Some of you added written material, moral support and overall encouragement to complete the task I had set out to do. You are very special to me in a way that only we know. I thank you so very much.

My special thanks goes to my wife Betty and our children Chris, Tim and Susan. I can only say thank you for your love, support and patience as I would disappear into the basement to work on my hobby and project. You mean so much to me. I love you.

To my support-tech writer and now new friend Meredy Shortal, Wow ! If you had only known the load of work I would put on you. I must say, in the spirit of your Marine Corps family, you came through with the quality of a top Marine. Thank you.

To my photographer and friend, Chris Mayberry of Mayberry Associates, Atlanta, GA., thank you. Chris, you gave new meaning to the word "quality" and this book is as good as it is because you were your own worst critic and would not accept anything less than what was right. You are a real professional in the industry.

To Nancy and Peter Schiffer, only because you gave me the support and continuing understanding is this book completed in 1995. You are outstanding and I thank you for your patience.

I would like to say thank you to the people who run the great collectible shows all over America such as the Scott's shows in Atlanta, Georgia, and Columbus, Ohio, and the Lakewood Antique and Collectible Show and the Pride of Dixie Show, also in Atlanta, Georgia. This type of show, along with the great Brimfield, Massachusetts, and the Webster, Florida, shows are such great resources to those of us who collect. They always seem to provide one more great item for a collection. I mention these because I frequent these more than others but have in fact visited shows and flea markets in over thirty states and five foreign countries.

I also would like to mention the wonderful antique mall operators as well as those who consign their treasures at these locations. And a special thanks goes to the thousands of individuals at antiques and collectibles shops throughout America. You do serve a great need beyond just economical value.

Thanks, too, to organizations such as the Ohio Valley Military Society that puts on shows that are just great for the American public. These shows continue to keep alive memories of units, branches of service and events that have occurred in history at such trying times. You fulfill a part in maintaining the history of war and what it has meant to all who have served or have an interest in preserving this great history. I thank you so very much. Also, my thanks goes to the organizations such as ASMIC, the American Society of Metal Insignia Collectibles. The service you provide in documenting and recording history will preserve our heritage for all mankind.

Yury and Isabella Altshuller
W. Hartford, CT

Mo Armstrong
Austin, TX

Richard G. Baade
Martinville, IN

Larry and Denise Baker
Tallahassee, FL

Dennis Blair
Abilene, KS

Pat Boarders
S. Carolina

Pete Bucholz
Lubbock, TX

John M. Burke
DeLand, FL

Ron Burkey
Portsmouth, NH

Donna Browning
Atlanta, GA

Pam Coghlan
Rutherford, NJ

Dave Collins
Panama Canal

Ray Connolly,
Edgewood, MD

Tom Cook
Atlanta, GA

Knowles B. Cornwell
Dallas, TX

William J. Crosby
Perrysberg, OH

Adela and Mike Crusco
Mt. Dora, FL

John Dahlstrom
Findley, OH

Carol Dalrymple
Atlanta, GA

Dan Daniel
Atlanta, GA

Doug Davis
Atlanta, GA

Dpt. Chief Wesley Derrick
Atlanta, GA

Lois "Cookie" Devine
Cincinnati, OH

Michelle Dyas
Roswell, GA

John Edwards
Chicopee, MD

Bill Erlewine
New Martinsville, W. VA

Mike Faiella
Brooklyn, NY

Jack Faubion
Tucker, GA

Susanne Faust
Atlanta, GA

Bill Finkler
Van Nuys, CA

John Gallia
Actworth, GA

Edwin Girrior
Haverhill, MA

Steve Griffith
Atlanta, GA

Joe Groseclose
Kingsport, TN

Lisa Holmes
Stamford, CT

Jere Hook
Roswell, GA

Bill and Alice Hurlbutt
Chicago, IL

Carol Iassogna
Huntington, CT

Dolores Isham
Keller, TX

J&L (Jules) Antiques
Edgemont, PA

Pat Jacob
Woodinville, WA

Kenneth D. Kaplan
Satellite Beach, FL

Jim and Glenna Knight
Lakeland, FL

Walter and Merle Koester
Ashville, NC

Patricia Koester-Smith
Norcross, GA

Robert Kopecny
Berwyn, IL

Nancy Lane
Jerome, ID

Sibyl Langley
Atlanta, GA

Ed Leavitt
Groveland, MS

Mr. Leonard
Atlanta, GA

Art Livingston
Brunswick, NJ

Jan and Chris Long
Bristol, VA

Frank Love
Long Beach, CA

Kathleen MacDonald
Lansing, MI

Mel Malenski
Baltimore, MD

Larry Martin
Middletown, VA

George Mattor
Oxford, MA

Chris Mayberry
Atlanta, GA

Carol Mehler
Bethel, PA

Merle Moen
Pinellas Pk., FL

Bob and Betty Morgan
Asheville, NC

Jerry and Debro Murray
Jacksonville, AL

Larry Noder
Odessa, FL

Greg and Ko Notarpole
Phoenix, AZ

Steve and Flo Pupek
St. Petersburg, FL

Earl Reed
Atlanta, GA

Gilmer Reynolds
Greensboro, NC

Joe Roscoe
Pennsylvania

Blake Shane
N. Hollywood, CA

Meredy Shortal
Atlanta, GA

Arnold & Joyce Simpson
Belleair Bluffs, FL

Colleen Simpson
Santa Monica, CA

Robert, Susan, & Trisha Smith
Mayville, WI

Betty Snider
Atlanta, GA

Chris Snider
Roswell, GA

Susan Snider
Atlanta, GA

Tim Snider
Atlanta, GA

Warren Snider
San Diego, CA

Randy and Cecilia Sheffield
Riverdale, GA

Ed and Shirley Stroble
Fairfield, OH

Stephen Werneth
Mobile, AL

Tony and Linda Wimmer
Foley, AL

PREFACE

Collecting keepsake items is an activity common to many people throughout the world since the beginning of time. The recognition of a loved one and, more importantly, that of a sweetheart, strikes a deep sentimental chord in each of us. To be able to wear or hold or visably display something that represents a loved one was a way to tell the world that you cared.

The practice of having a keepsake for a family member grew in the United States significantly during the period from 1917 to 1919 as our world entered into one of the most devastating wars in the history of mankind. The creation of pins, bracelets, buttons, banners, plaques, flags, posters, pins, cards, necklaces, lockets and many other items gave to those dealing with war on the Home Front something with which to honor their loved ones while also showing patriotism for their country.

This book was written to preserve a unique piece of our history and great heritage. This document will allow all present and future citizens throughout the world to appreciate the depth to which our love and support of our heroes was displayed.

Today, collecting sweetheart jewelry and keepsake items is rapidly gaining a following. There is great opportunity for one to enter into this world of special items that bear so much history and romance.

Why was sweetheart jewelry so important? Besides the obvious display of patriotism and loyalty by the wearer, sweetheart jewelry offered new possibilities in fashion that were in line with wartime rationing.

During the war, government regulation challenged the fashion industry by strictly limiting the fabric a civilian manufacturer might use: no more than two inches of hem; no more than one patch-pocket per blouse; no attached hoods or shawls; no skirt more than seventy-two inches around; no belts more than two inches wide; no cuffs on coats. Sweetheart jewelry that included lockets, pins, pilot's wings, necklaces, pendants, earrings, bracelets and rings were accessories that took on a supreme significance in overcoming the skimpy wartime look. American women happily accessorized their spartan suits, scanty skirts, and unpocketed, ruffleless blouses knowing they were quite correct going to work or hoeing their Victory garden. Sweetheart jewelry became another great example of American ingenuity in a time of overwhelming shortages.

There were so many manufacturers of these items that it is difficult, if not impossible, to list all of their identities now. On the other hand, many items were handmade and one of a kind.

The value guide in the back of this book is presented only as a guide and is not the final word on prices. Too many variable factors are present to be definitive: geography, fragility, personal preference and the whims of dealers and collectors in the marketplace are a few. Only the buyer or seller will possess pricing ability. However, in general prices have been making a steady climb as more people recognize this wonderful opportunity to collect and protect our history.

To date, a lot of information has been written on military uniforms, firearms, headgear, emblems, paper items, and military issue items but collecting keepsakes and sweetheart jewelry presents something different, the human side of warfare. Keepsake items remind us that wars were fought by human beings. Jewelry and collectibles are proof that war extends beyond the battlefield and help us realize just how much the lives of large numbers of civilians and non-combatants were significantly altered as they worked together for the survival of our free world.

A representative look at some of the many different types of jewelry from the early Forties up to the mid-Fifties. Plastics, Lucite and hard metal were commonly used along with mother-of-pearl, glass, leather and wood. Finding items in their original containers or on original cards is rare and they will always command higher prices.

A patriotic poster that tells so much to the reader. From rank designations to service branches to cost for a pair of shoes, much can be learned about the collectibles in this book by studying its sections. Circa 1943.

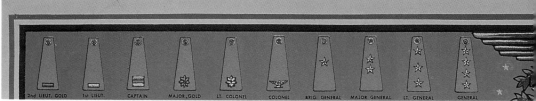

GLOSSARY

A.A.F.- Army Air Force

A.E.F.- American Expeditionary Force (1917-1919)

Bas-relief- Slight pattern projection on a flat surface.

Bevel- Sloping angle of a surface.

Celluloid- Trademark thermoplastic material used as substitute or ivory, horn, or tortoise shell.

Chasing- Ornamental metal work using engraving or embossing techniques.

Chatelaine- Ornamental chain hung from a brooch or belt, from which small objects are suspended.

Chevron- "V"-shaped bars or lines.

Cloisonne- Fused powdered glass placed in separate case cells formed from thin stripes of metal.

Compact- Small cosmetic case containing face powder and/or rouge and a mirror.

Ebonite- Black variety of vulcanized rubber capable of being cut and polished.

Embossing- Carved or hammered design that is raised above a flat surface.

Engine-Turning- Ornamental engraving done by machinery.

Filigree- Lace-like ornamental metal work.

Goldtone- Any gold colored metallic finish.

High-Relief- Sculptured figures which project by more than half from background.

Incising- Engraving or carving into a flat surface with a sharp tool.

Kamra- Case resembling early collapsible camera cases.

Logo- A word, letter, symbol, or character representing an entire phrase or name.

Lucite- Trademark name for acrylic or material, high translucency.

Lunette- Crescent shaped.

Marcasite- A staple stone of costume jewelry, a crystallized piece of a whitish-yellow mineral that has been cut and polished.

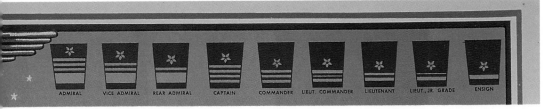

Mizpah- Means "watchtower" and is derived from a parting salutation in Genesis xxi 49.

M.O.P.- Mother of Pearl- hard pearly interior layer of certain marine shells.

Nickel Silver- Hard alloy of nickel, copper, and zinc.

Passementerie- Heavy fabric trimming usually of gold or silver gimp, cord, or braid.

Pendant- Suspended from a chain or ring.

Pewter- Dull silvery-gray alloy of tin and lead.

Plexiglas- Trademark name for synthetic resins.

Porcelain- Hard white nonporous variety of ceramic ware.

Repoussé- Decoration achieved by pushing out the metal into relief by reverse tooling.

Reverse- The exterior back of an object.

Rhinestone- Artificial gem made of glass.

Silvertone- Any silver colored metallic finish.

SPAR- A member of the Women's Reserve of the United States Coast Guard Reserve. From the initials of the Coast Guard motto, "Semper Paratus, Always Ready."

Sterling- Standard pure silver with minute variable alloys.

USA- United States Army, United States of America

USAF- United States Air Force

USCG- United States Coast Guard

USMC- United States Marine Corps

USN- United States Navy

Vermeil- Gilded silver or white metal.

WAAC- U.S. Women's Army Auxiliary Corps (the former name of the Women's Army Corps or WAC).

WAVE- A woman in the United States Navy other than a nurse. From the initials of the descriptive title, Women Accepted for Volunteer Emergency Service.

White Metal- Generic term for any unidentified silver looking metal composition.

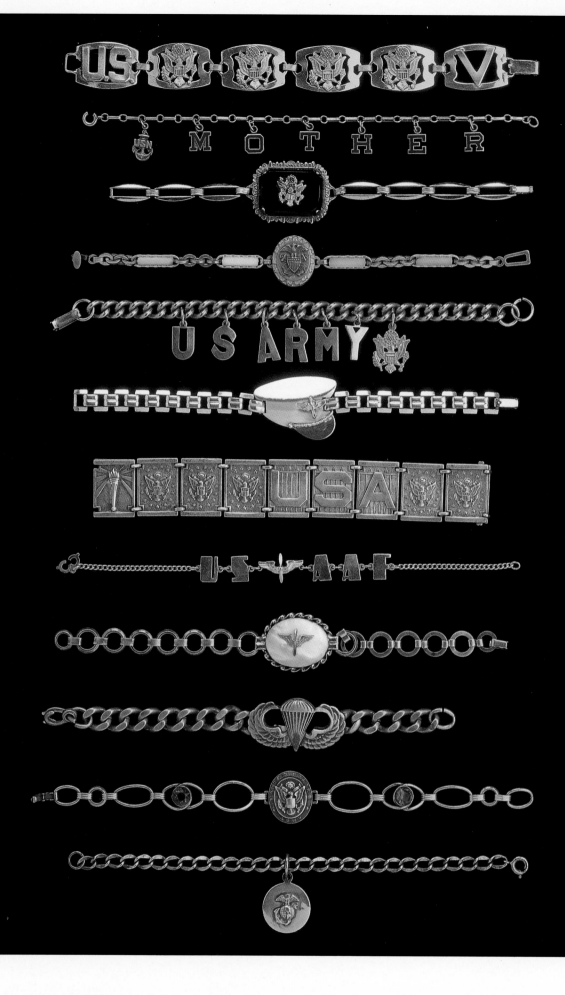

BRACELETS

One of the largest groups of military sweetheart jewelry is bracelets. They were worn by both men and women as a recognizable display of patriotism that showed both love of country and love of a family member.

Early military bracelets appear to have originated from the forget-me-not bracelets of the 1930s. These attractive link bracelets were usually composed of sterling silver. Variations appeared during the Allied Campaign through Italy during WW II. A local craftsman or professional jeweler would insert a military link in the center of a forget-me-not bracelet.

The variety of materials used to make these bracelets will never cease to amaze the Sweetheart collector. In addition to nickel silver, German silver, silverplate, 14k, 10k, sterling and hardcast metals, there are also bracelets made from black onyx, mother-of-pearl, Lucite and ivory. Bracelets in this collection are also made of coins, buttons, a WW II cannon shell, and a combat infantry badge.

Bracelets were generally worn by a husband, wife, girlfriend, or boyfriend. They became prominent during World Wars I and II. Today, there are very few bracelets in the market place recognizing the Korean or Vietnam conflicts.

Among the many types of bracelets displayed in this book are ones with lockets, charms, molded shapes, flex bands, plastic parts, flags and handmade varieties.

The locket bracelet usually had a heart in the center that was suitable for carrying a small picture. The heart may have a military insignia or a division or battalion designation.

Charm bracelets were very popular and some would spell out a branch of the service such as USAF, USN, US ARMY or the camp or post at which the soldier was stationed. Charms could also spell out a member of the family, such as "Mother."

Molded bracelets sometimes were handmade from a combat infantry badge, military emblems, a pilot's, gunner's, navigator's or bombadier's wings, sea shell products, Lucite windshields and the aluminum of downed fighter aircraft.

Flex band bracelets generally displayed a military branch of the service. Plastics and Lucite bracelets are not common because, in many cases, these bracelets were made from the windshield materials; most of them have an Air Force or Marine emblem set into the design. Many of these bracelets appear to be a part of "Pacific War Art" which was handmade on islands in the Pacific Ocean region.

Flag bracelets were colorful and very attractive. They could show the flags of the Allied nations or display signal flags spelling out the name of a ship such as the "USS Washington".

Handmade bracelets are represented in a series of China/Burma/India bracelets predominantly in sterling silver. They are hand painted, very colorful and, in this collection, have the military US Army CBI insignia.

When discussing handmade bracelets, it is important to mention "Pacific War Art" of the 1940s, a category similar to "Trench Art" from the First World War. Military personnel overseas would fill up lonely hours making jewelry to send a message of love to someone back home. They would pound, mold, hammer, and polish any available piece of metal or plastic into a piece of jewelry. Many aluminum collectibles can be found with dates, the location, and the name of the artist.

An original box with a Coast Guard bracelet and chain. Circa 1942. Also pictured is a pin and necklace set from the U. S. Navy on an original card. Circa 1940s.

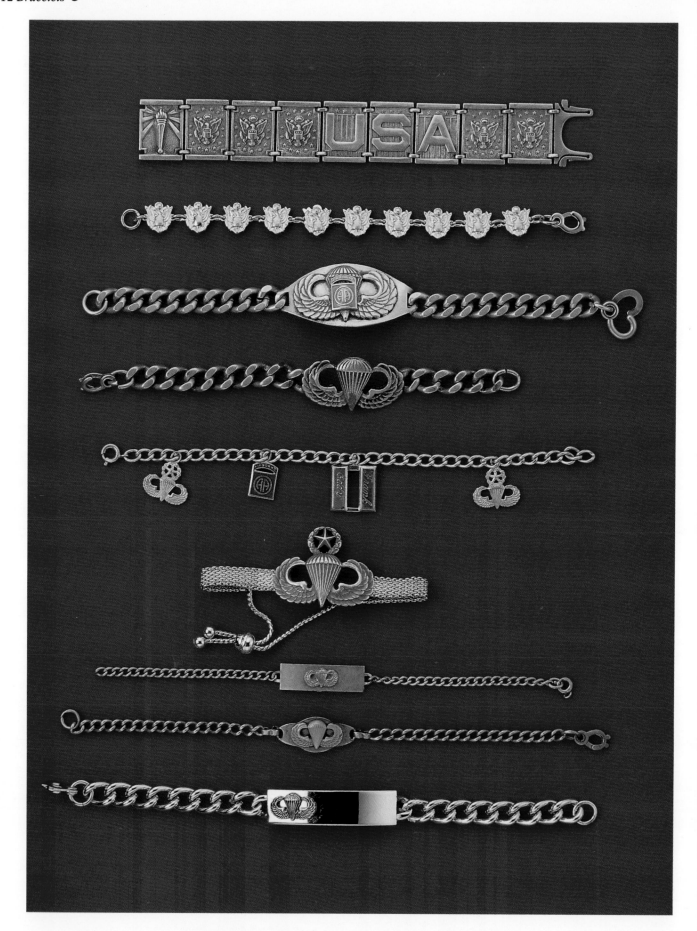

Bracelets made from sterling silver to pot metal and gold and silver plate.
Paratrooper wings are on several pieces.

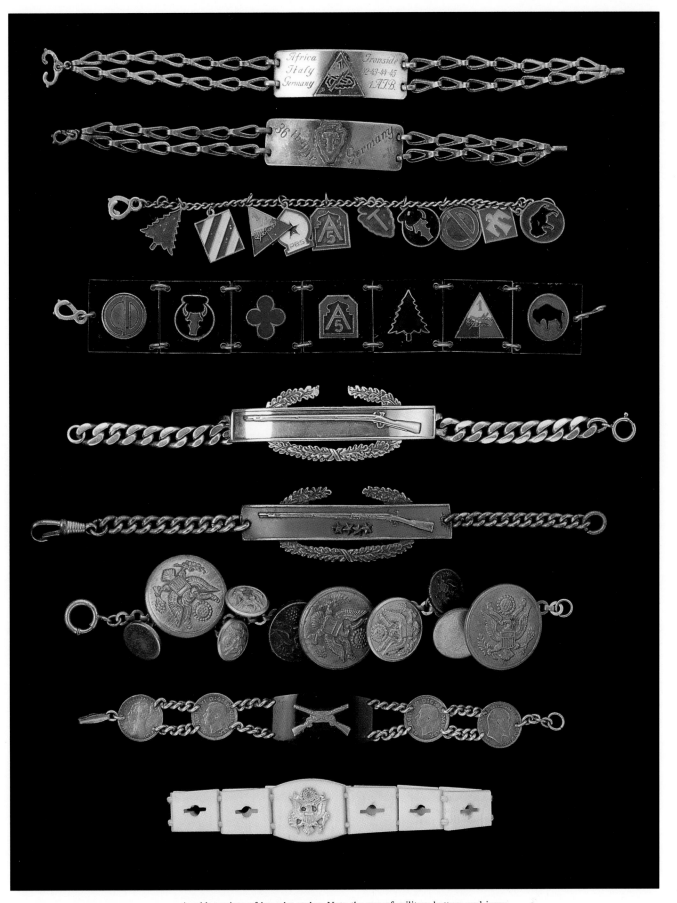

A wide variety of bracelet styles. Note the use of military buttons and ivory. Hand made bracelets created from Army combat infantry badges (long rifle on bar) show what soldiers could create. This group ranges from the 1940s to 1950s.

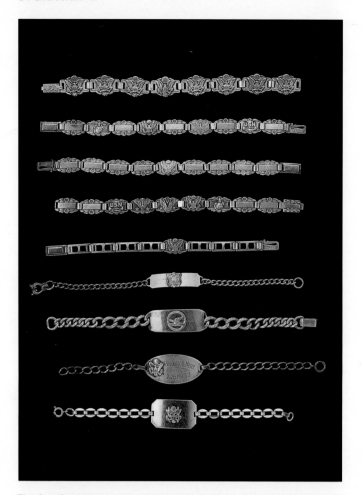

The four forget-me-not bracelets shown at the top were popular from the early 1900s to 1945. Most forget-me-not bracelets are sterling silver. The identification bracelets with a central solid bar, and commonly referred to as "I.D. bracelets," were popular to all branches of the service.

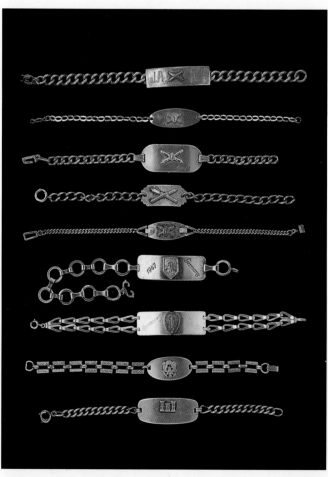

I. D. bracelets showing the many types of links used as well as different items attached to the bar such as cannons, castles, rifles and a multitude of other insignia. Circa 1940 - 1955.

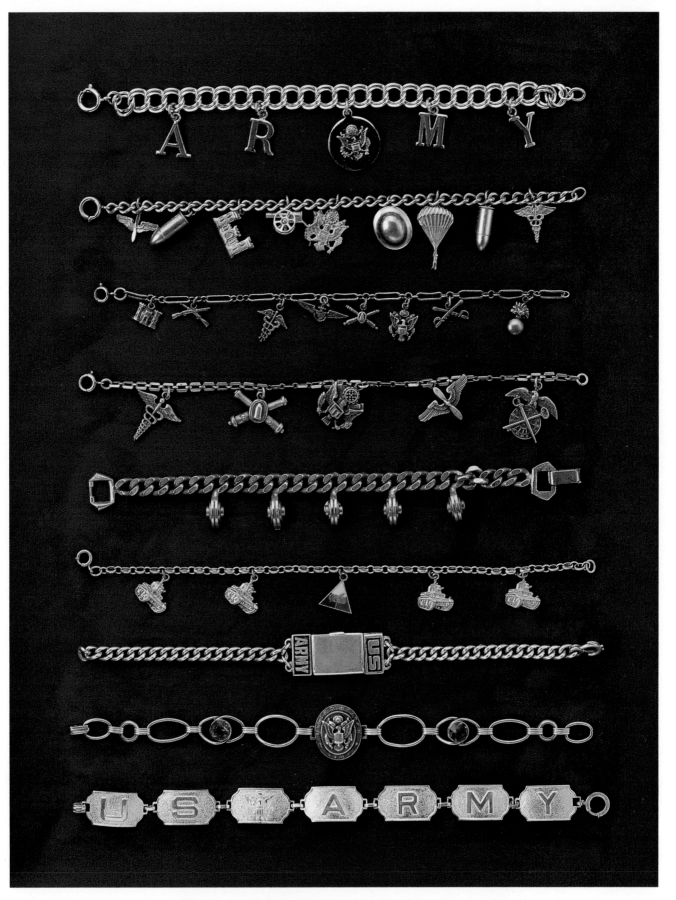

The charm bracelet was popular with all branches of the military as well as with civilians. This beautiful selection represents the U. S. Army. Sterling silver as well as both gold plate and silver plate are common materials for these bracelets. Circa 1940 - 1955.

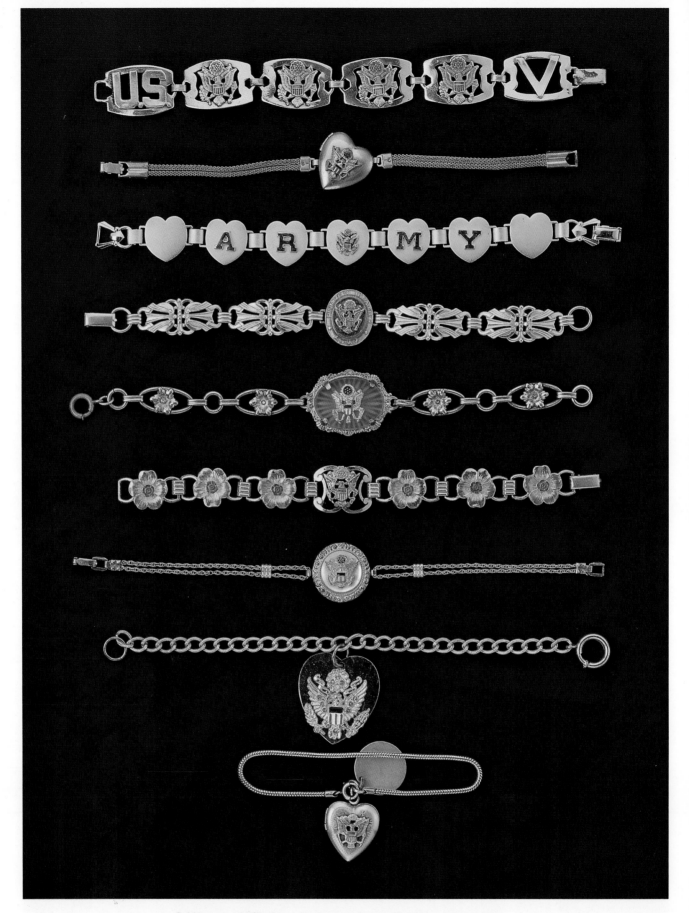

Goldtone or gold-filled bracelets representing the U. S. Army showed just
how creative manufacturers could be in their appeal to buyers during 1940
to 1955.

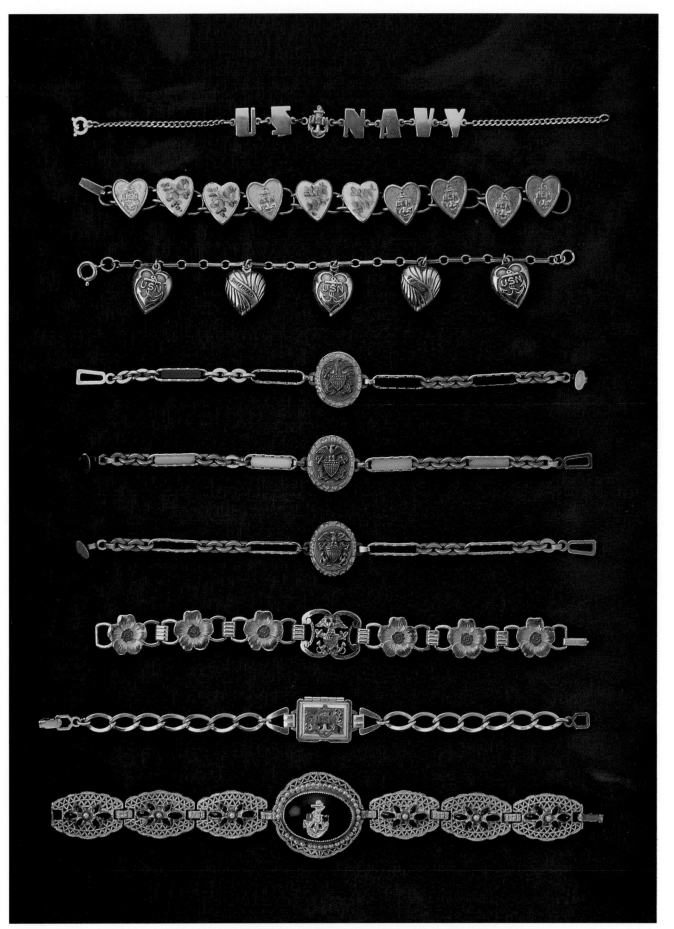

For the U. S. Navy, many designs of bracelets were made. From letters and
words to hearts and flowers, these represent the 1940 to 1945 era.

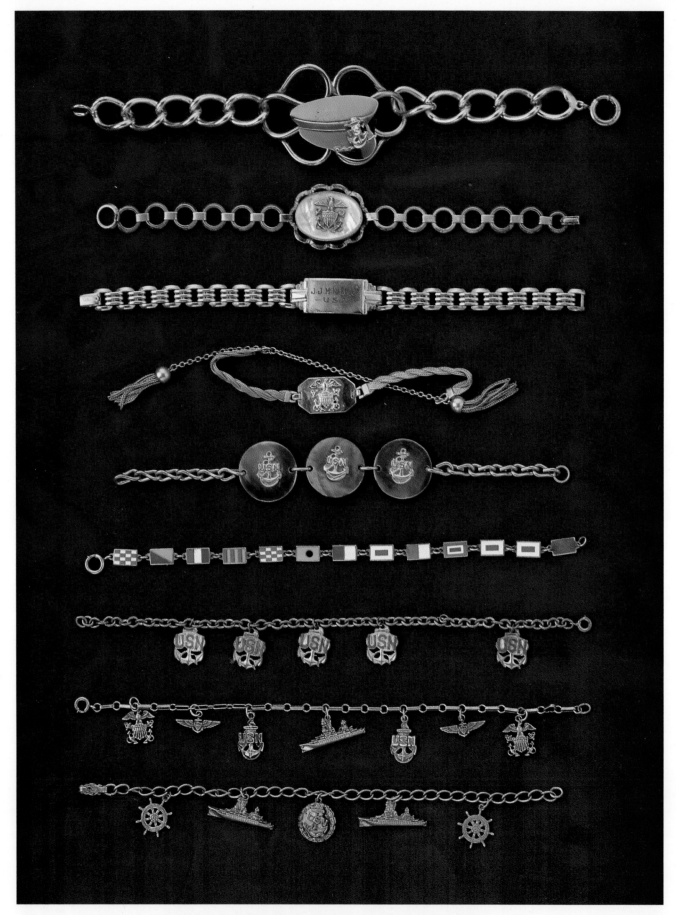

U. S. Navy bracelets showing various insignia from hats to ships and anchors. The signal flag bracelet indicates the U.S.S. Washington. The charm bracelets were popular with all services. Circa 1940 to 1945.

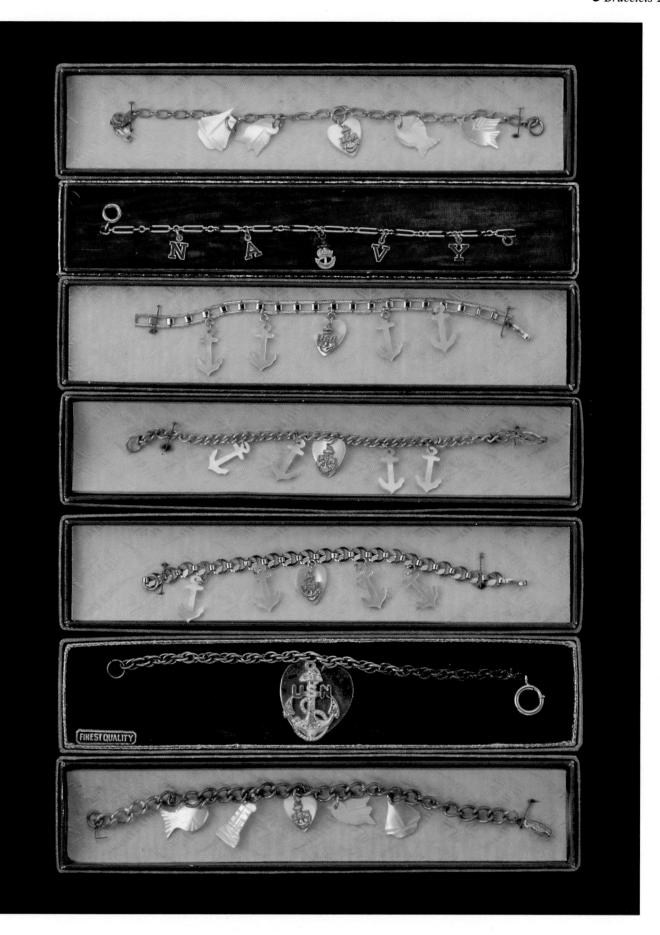

U. S. Navy bracelets with charms made from sea shells in their original
boxes are a rare find. This group will command higher prices. Circa 1940 -
1945.

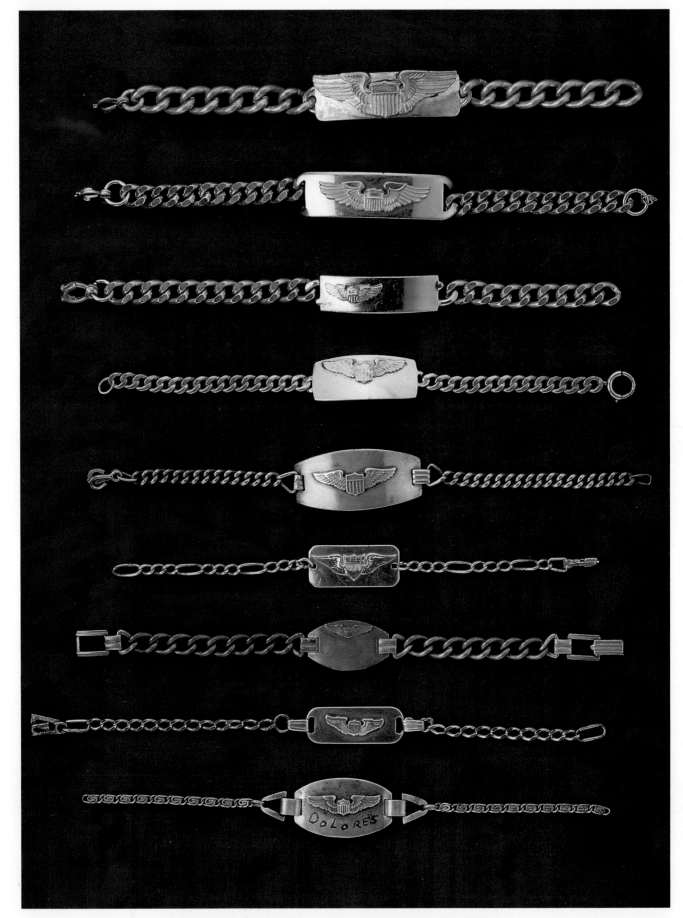

I. D. bracelets representing the U. S. Navy were very popular. On occasion, an inscription will be etched on the under side of the bar. All the bracelets shown here are pilot wings from the 1940s to 1950s.

I. D. bracelets were among the least expensive type of bracelet manufactured during the war years. The I. D. bracelet was very popular and may have had the name of a loved one engraved on it. Circa 1915 to 1950.

The varied sizes of I. D. bracelets can be seen clearly in this group as well as the use of gold insignia on silver bars and silver insignia on gold bars, 1940s to 1950s.

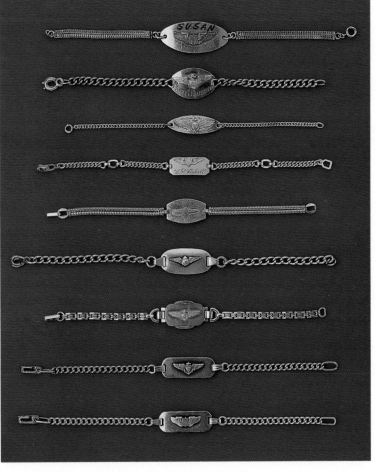

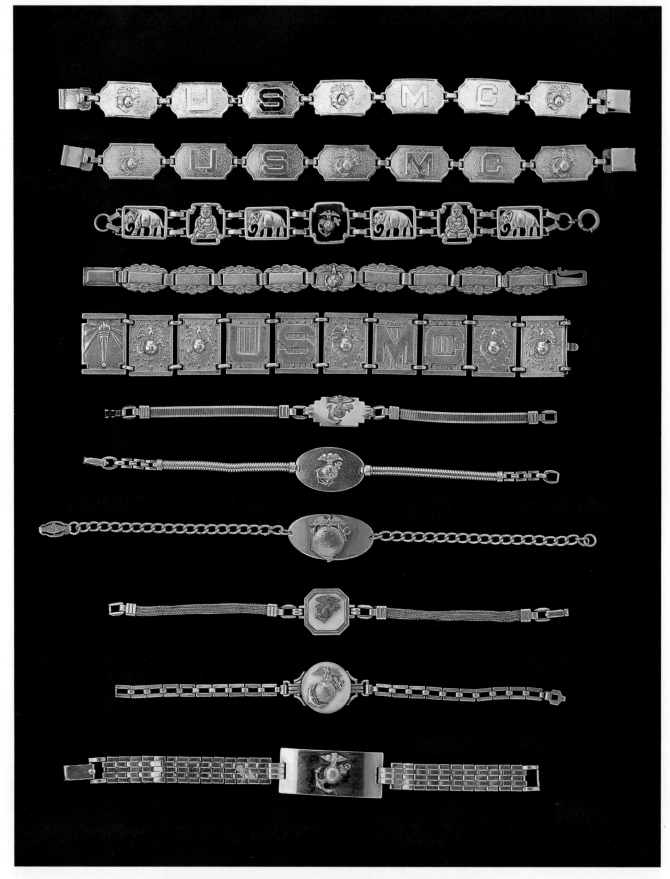

Marine Corps bracelets are not common. The prices will generally be higher for Marine Corps items in all areas. The bracelet showing the elephants is very unusual as most Marine Corps items have only the emblems on them. USMC, for the United States Marine Corps, is a common abbreviation for "The Corps," circa 1940 - 1945.

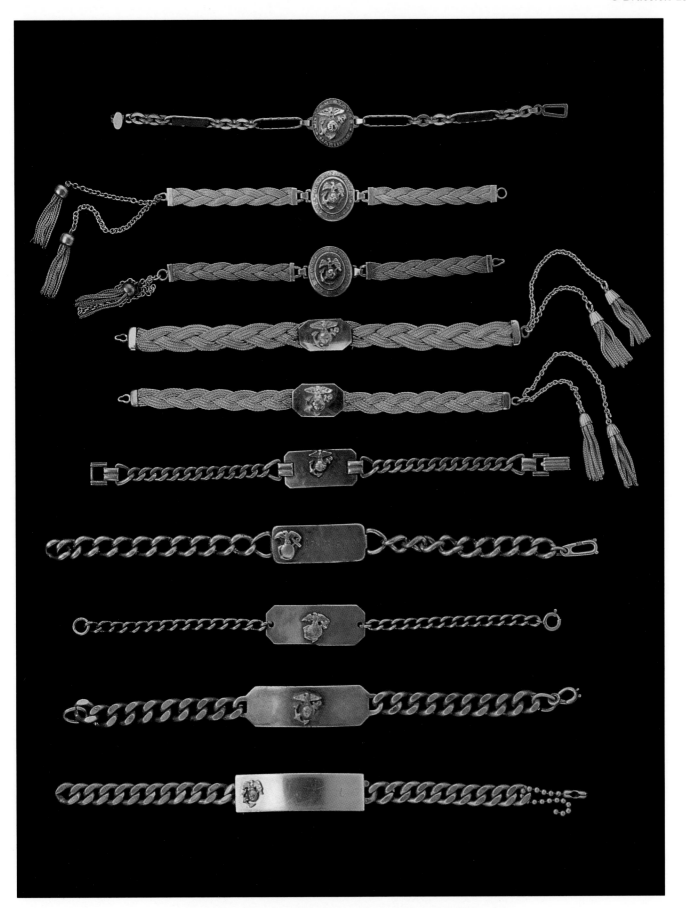

U. S. Marine Corps bracelets could be just as ornate and beautiful as those made for any other service branch. The gold colored bracelets with the woven wire bands and rat-tail hanging chains are among the most attractive items. Circa 1940s to 1953.

U. S. Air Force bracelets have wings with a propeller, the most common
identification for this branch of service. The hand made bracelets shown at
the top and bottom indicate the wide variety produced. Circa 1940 to 1945.

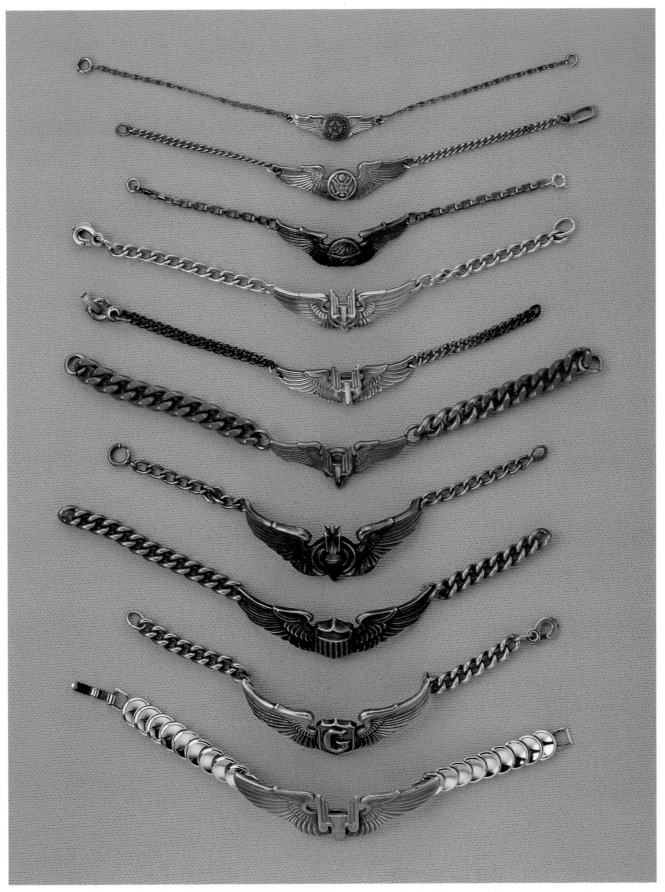

Creating your own bracelet from a regulation set of wings or from a miniature set could easily be done with the U. S. Air Force wings. The many
different types of links and locking devices are shown in this group, 1940 to
1950s.

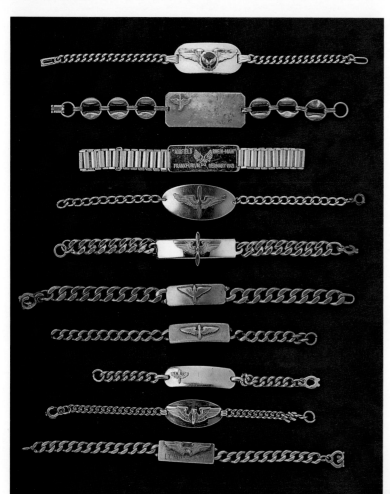

The U. S. A. C., United States Air Corps, was also known in its early times as the A. A. F., Army Air Force. The U. S. Air Force was created as a stand-alone branch in 1947. This group of bracelets date circa 1940 to 1945.

The I. D. bracelet style was also very popular with the Air Force members and their loved ones. This group shows the many varied styles of wings used to signify the Air Force in the 1940s and beyond.

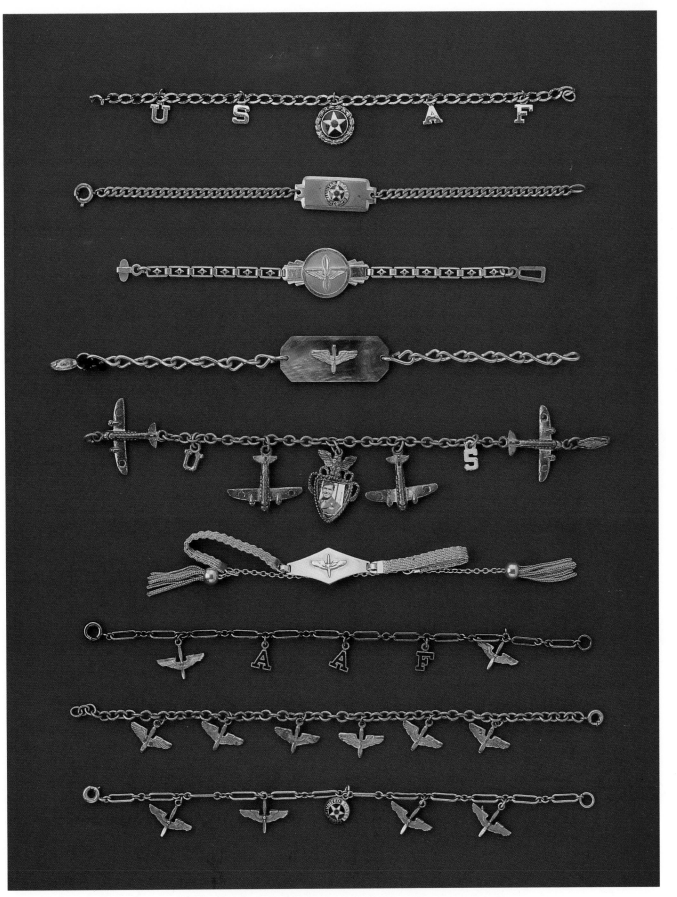

U. S. Air Force charm bracelets were another popular style carried over from civilian use. The use of letters, wings and planes as charms was common. The gold-toned bracelet in the middle has a high quality, rich appearance. Circa 1940 - 1945.

The handmade Lucite bracelets on the left are very rare and many are one-of-a-kind. Represented from top to bottom are the U. S. Navy, Air Force, Marine Corps, Air Force and Army. The beautiful flex band bracelets on the right side were commercially manufactured. Circa 1940 -1945.

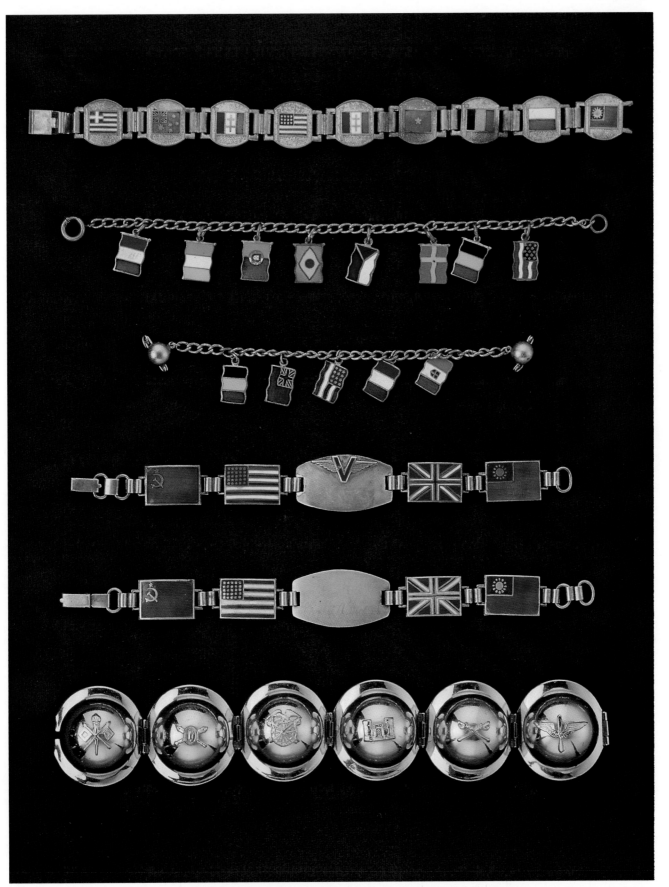

The first five bracelets with flags represent the Allied powers. The fourth bracelet from the top is very rare and has the flags of the Big Four Allied powers: Russia, United States, Great Britain and China, as well as a "V" (for Victory) on the bar. The bracelet at the bottom is a very rare item made with links in the shape of helmets with different service emblems on top.

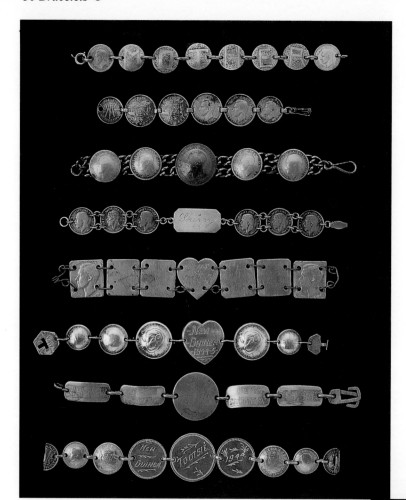

Handmade bracelets shown here depict either Trench Art, that was created during the war in Europe, or Pacific War Art, that was created on an island or aboard ship in the South Pacific Ocean during World War II. The bracelets here are made from coins or other metals.

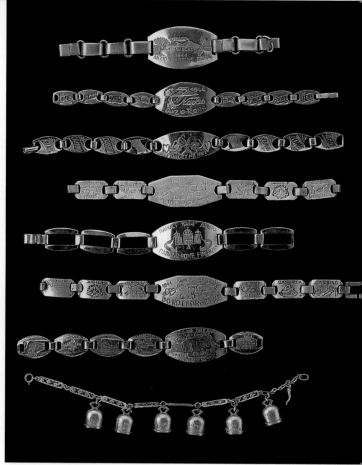

Bracelets made by hand either by a G.I. (U. S. soldier) or citizens of Italy around 1944.

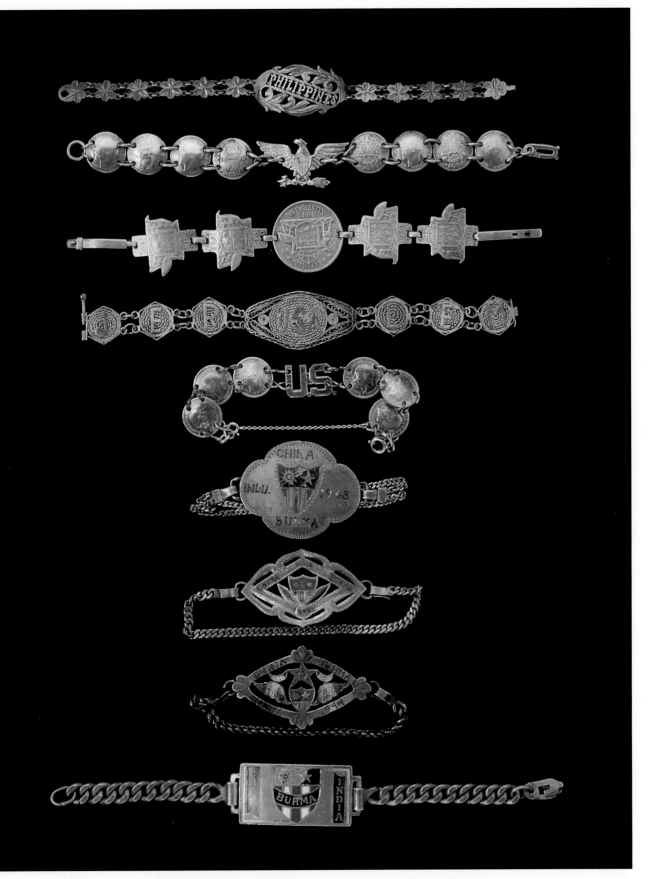

Handmade bracelets made during the Second World War in the Pacific
Theater are referred to as Pacific War Art. Other examples of handmade
bracelets appeared during the war in China, Burma, and India. The "C. B. I."
type bracelets with painted enamels are among the most colorful and command the highest prices today. Some have sold for hundreds of dollars.

COMPACTS
CIGARETTE CASES
MIRRORS
PICTURE HOLDERS

Made to sell during World War II, military compacts were intensely personal and showed their own style of patriotic commitment. For example, in 1945, Naval Midshipman (later President) Jimmy Carter gave his fiancee a compact for Christmas. The initials engraved on the the top, "ILYTG," were a favorite Carter family inscription for "I love you the goodest."

Compacts in this collection generally display a military emblem or designate a military installation. The Navy is represented by an anchor. Some Navy compacts have an officer's insignia which is an eagle resting on a shield of crossed anchors. Other Navy categories include dolphins in water with a submarine slicing through it representing the submarine group, pilot's wings with an anchor, and the letters USN depicting naval aviation.

The Air Force compacts display an eagle over a shield. Aviation is represented by wings with a single propeller blade through it.

The Marine Corps compacts have an eagle over a globe and anchor.

The Army compacts will be recognized by a lone eagle and the words "US Army" may be written below it. Further subdivisions by branches of the service include twin towers for the Corps of Engineers, crossed rifles for the Infantry, and crossed flags for the Signal Corps.

The Coast Guard compacts show crossed anchors with a shield in the center. Generally, the words "United States Coast Guard" will be written in a circle around the emblem.

Military compacts can truly be a joy to collect. Whimsical compacts can be found shaped like a camera or military headgear. Other shapes include hearts, squares, ovals and rectangular pieces. A limited number of compacts in this collection have manufacturing identification on them, such as Evans, Elgin American, Zell, Bonita Volupte, and Henriette and Girey, who was one of the primary manufacturers of camera compacts during the war.

The only World War I compact in this collection has "AEF" on the top of a red, white and blue shield representing the American Expeditionary Force. Two of the compacts shown are British and this is not surprising. In 1941, "Bundles for Britain" was a popular social charity and volunteers opened a boutique in New York selling purse accessories with British flags or regimental crests to raise war relief funds. Macy's department store supported the Battle of Britain heroes by selling compacts with a Royal Air Force insignia.

Military compacts were frequently purchased by servicemen at the base PX's for special events, sweetheart, family, or special occasion mementos and they were available through the Sears Roebuck catalogue. Compacts were given as souvenirs of

the military academies, such as the one shown in this collection with "USMA" (United States Military Academy) for West Point. Also shown are compacts made as souvenirs of countries such as Japan and Korea.

The sizes of military compacts vary from 1.25 inches to 4 inches across. It was usual for the compacts to have two interior compartments, one for rouge and one for loose powder.

Materials used in making these compacts included metal, wood, mother-of-pearl, leather, brass, polished tin, wood combinations, sterling and gold filled silver, mesh chain, and plastic. In 1942, the beginning of the war caused major upheavals in the United States cosmetic industry with restrictions against metals for cosmetic use. A "make-do" spirit launched the popularity of newer resin plastics such as Lucite and plexiglas. It became a patriotic gesture to buy and carry plastic accessories.

Some military compacts were hand-crafted of wood with flip-lock levers or leather with zippered closures, but most were manufactured. Some were plain while others were elaborate with engravings or rhinestones. Some compacts have been preserved in dresser drawers in their original boxes while others were "well worn." But in retrospect, all of them, regardless of condition, combined usefulness with a sentiment of patriotic commitment.

Collecting cigarette cases and smoking accessories has become a widespread hobby enjoyed by both men and women. This section will highlight four military cigarette cases that show the versatility of their designs.

Military cigarette cases were popular as souvenirs. During World War II, it became popular to depict countries, routes or branches of the service on the faces of smoking accessories. Pictured in this section is a unique and interesting example of "Trench Art." The largest cigarette case is handcrafted out of aluminum with hand carved designs on four sides, inside and outside. A kneeling woman is on the front, a soldier kissing a girl under a lamp post is on the back. Inside are connecting heart cutouts suitable for inserting a picture, and various symbols of Egypt.

The second largest cigarette case is made of silver metal and has over 25 different military emblems mounted to the front and back. They range from service stars, Red Cross, In-service and efficiency pins, to a British button, unit insignia, and a World War I armor emblem.

Also featured is a sterling silver 1920s case to which a US Air Force wing insignia has been added. Also, there is an expandable cigarette pack protector case with an Air Force bomber centered on the front.

In the marketplace, a collector may find a popular combination case and lighter by Evans or a wooden case that features

a sliding top which reveals cylinders for 10 individual cigarettes.

Cigarette cases also can be found in precious metals such as sterling silver, platinum and gold. Naturally, these command higher prices than cases of brass, cloth, wood, chromium, rhodium, or nickel plate.

Manufacturers of Sweetheart cigarette cases include Evans, Longines and Alfred Dunhill of London, one of the most respected names in smoking accessories.

The U. S. Army compacts shown here. Circa 1940-1945, have plastic covers as well as jeweled, imprinted, and enamel painted designs. Military compacts are not common and will command high prices.

Small mirrors were a popular military keepsake item. Many had pictures on one side that were laminated to tin. Others were made of fabric and had sayings such as "Remember Me USA," "Sweetheart USA," and "Wife USA."

From 1910 to 1945, "Kamara" style compacts that resembled a collapsible camera were very popular. They open by pushing a spring-loaded button and releasing the top. An Army insignia is attached to each of these except the one in the lower left which has a shield with initials "A.E.F." for American Expeditionary Force, which was a reference used during World War I.

U. S. Army compacts embossed with the shield of the Great Seal of the
United States and painted with red, white and blue were both colorfully
symbolic and patriotic. Circa 1940 - 1945.

Headgear compacts were made to resemble items of military use and were novelties during the war years. All branches of service are represented. The dark green compact on the left and the white compact on the right are made from plastics while the others are gold-toned metal.

U. S. Navy compacts showing hearts were very popular. The compact with
a mother-of-pearl appearance and an officer's emblem is a rare find. The
"Kamara" style compact could be found in all branches of the service.

U. S. Marine Corps compacts are among the hardest to find. The compact
showing the Marine Corps hat and emblem is very rare. Nearly every U. S.
Marine Corps compact has the emblem only. Circa 1940 - 1945.

Shown are U. S. Air Force and Army Air Corps compacts. The emblem of wings with a propeller identifies it as Air Force. The wooden compact in the upper fight has a flip lock which was clever but not practical as the lock would fail and the mirror could break. Circa 1940 - 1950.

Air Force or Army Air Force compacts also come in the form of a "Kamara" style compact. The two lower compacts with black surfaces and goldtone wings are highly collectible.

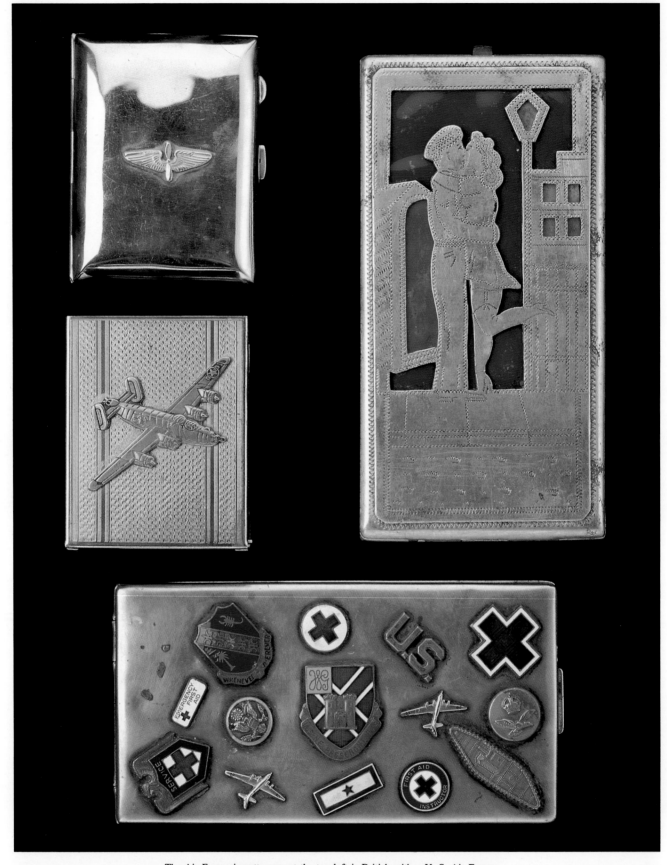

The Air Force cigarette case at the top left is British with a U. S. Air Force emblem. The cigarette case with the American bomber image on it was manufactured by the Dunhill Co. The back of the cigarette case at the center bottom is sterling silver with thirteen different emblems. The cigarette case at the upper right is handmade, hand tooled and one-of-a-kind with a place for pictures inside (not shown). Circa 1940 -1945.

Shown are the backs of two cigarette cases shown opposite. The valuable hand tooled case shows a beautiful woman on the outside and (not shown) a desert scene with a pyramid and palm tree inside. The case with all the emblems is also rare and valuable. At the lower left is a rare sterling silver British compact. At the lower right is a moderately-priced plastic British compact.

Mirrors with an embroidered great seal of the United States or the emblem
of the U.S. Army on the back side were a novelty. These mirrors could be
purchased with mailer envelopes and sent back home to a wife, sweetheart,
mother or sister. Circa 1940 - 1945.

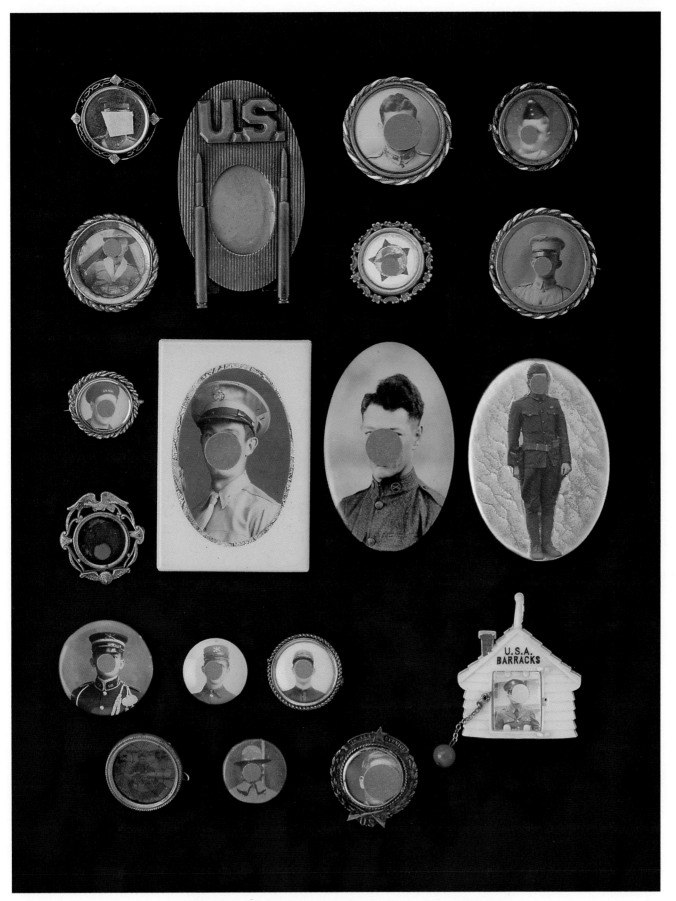

Picture frames and other picture holders of a service man or woman were popular during both World Wars I and II. Some would sit on a dresser while others had a mirror on the reverse side and would be carried in a pocket-book.

HANDKERCHIEFS
AND HOLDERS

Soldiers and sailors returning from the wars had only a limited opportunity to shop for something to take home to their mothers, wives, or sweethearts. One of the most popular items was the fancy, embroidered souvenir handkerchief. The themes generally featured a patriotic, sentimental, or location motif. Martial themes, ranging from ships to branches of the service, were also popular.

In the marketplace, the collector will see many handkerchiefs with a flag motif. When two flags are featured, one is generally that of a liberated country, and the second will be that of the liberating armed force.

This collection shows handkerchiefs that are souvenirs from England, France, and Korea. A single handkerchief easily can be valued at $10. A boxed set of three can be in the $20 range. Some boxed sets will have a dozen handkerchiefs in different colors such as yellow, purple, pink, and red.

Collectible handkerchiefs can be made of rayon, linen, and, in some cases, silk. In this collection, there are two World War I "Forget Me Not" silk handkerchiefs representing "Camp Logan the World's Democracy Defenders of 1917-18." On one, pictures of a soldier and a women frame the poem *Remember Me*:

Sweet be to thee life's passing hours.
And all thy paths be decked with flowers.

This handkerchief is bordered in a number of military emblems, the flag, crossed sabres, a cannon and crossed rifles. It's value is in the $20 range.

On rare occasions, a collector might find a handkerchief holder in the marketplace. These rectangular, satin cases often had a "Hello" or "Sweetheart" poem on the front. They generally have a padded construction featuring decorative cording and tassels. Their average price is in the $50 range.

This 1917 Camp Logan souvenir handkerchief with a picture of a soldier and his sweetheart is a type popular during World War I. Not many have survived to the present.

A colorful set of handkerchiefs showing "Mother" and "Sweetheart" could be mailed home as a gift for a loved one. This group is representative of the U. S. Army types. Circa 1940 - 1945.

This group of multi-colored handkerchiefs represents the Navy, Army and Army Air Force (prior to 1947). Circa 1940 - 1945.

Colorful sets of handkerchiefs that ranged from plain to fancy with embroidered military emblems could be purchased at retail stores and at military bases in boxes that could be mailed.

The "hankies" holder is an unusual item that dates back to the First World War. Many have beautiful verses written on them as well as colorful designs and emblems. These are much more expensive than handkerchiefs. Circa 1917 to 1945.

IN-SERVICE PINS

"She Wears a Star for a Man at War"

During World War II, there was a time of great personal sacrifice by mothers, fathers, wives, children and friends who saw their loved ones go off to war. One of the most popular and visible ways to display love and patriotism was to wear a "service star." A pin consisting of a blue star on a white background surrounded by a narrow, red border showed the world that a loved one was involved in the war effort. The design is the same as that of a service flag approved for display in windows or upon walls.

In-service pins were considered "The insignia of honor to the wearer," according to the fine print on the original cards to which the pins were attached. The most common In-service pins will have one star; pins with more than one star become more rare as the number of stars increases. Any number of stars beyond four will certainly be an exception and, no doubt, a real treasure. In some cases a gold star would signify that a loved one was deceased.

Collectors will find that the marketplace offers a great variety of these specialized pins. An In-service pin can be a simple bar pin, a bar pin with an attachment, an ornate brooch, or a pin that clearly designates a branch of the service or an individual unit within a branch of the service. They also can denote rank, the location of the serviceman (such as France) and in the case of one pin pictured in this section, religious affiliation.

Many of the Navy In-service pins in this section show an anchor with the initials "USN" above the star. The Army pins feature an American eagle. Often they will have an attachment of crossed rifles representing the Infantry, crossed cannons for the Field Artillery, wings with a propeller for the Air Forces, crossed flags for the Signal Corps or a caduceus for the Medical Corps.

The Marine Corps In-service pins will show an eagle, globe, and anchor. The Coast Guard will have an emblem that shows crossed anchors with a shield in the center. Generally the words, "United States Coast Guard" will be written in a circle around the emblem. The Air Force will show a pair of wings with an emblem of the US shield and the American eagle.

The In-service pins in this collection range in quality from Tiffany's to handcrafted. They can be obtained very inexpensively for five and six dollars, but values can climb to over a hundred dollars. At a recent antique show in Atlanta, Georgia, one dealer was offering a one star pin made of rubies and diamond chips for $950.

In-service pins can be found in the shapes of a heart, bell, shield, flag, diamond, circle, anchor, octagon, wings, and the most common -- a rectangular bar. They can designate a son, brother, sweetheart and, without question, a husband. They were originally intended to represent family members exclusively but a broader base evolved. One pin photographed in this collection has "boyfriend" written on it.

Materials used in the construction of In-service pins include, 14k gold, sterling silver, silver and gold metal alloys, enamel over metal, cloth, plastic, wood, and beads, just to name a few.

The In-service star is not restricted only to pins. Rings, pendants, buttons, bracelets, pillow covers, banners, flags and pennants, small picture frames, books and many other Home Front items had a visible star that signified that someone "near or dear" was serving the country.

Also in this section, are small service emblems that designated a branch of service and sometimes an individual unit within that branch, such as infantry. There was no star but the emblem represented the same pride and patriotism as the In-service pin. A WW I service emblem photographed on its original card has the verse:

> "As a token from me, I ask you to wear
> This small service emblem, please guard it with care.
> 'Twill remind you and others that I am away,
> Just doing my bit, for the old U.S.A."

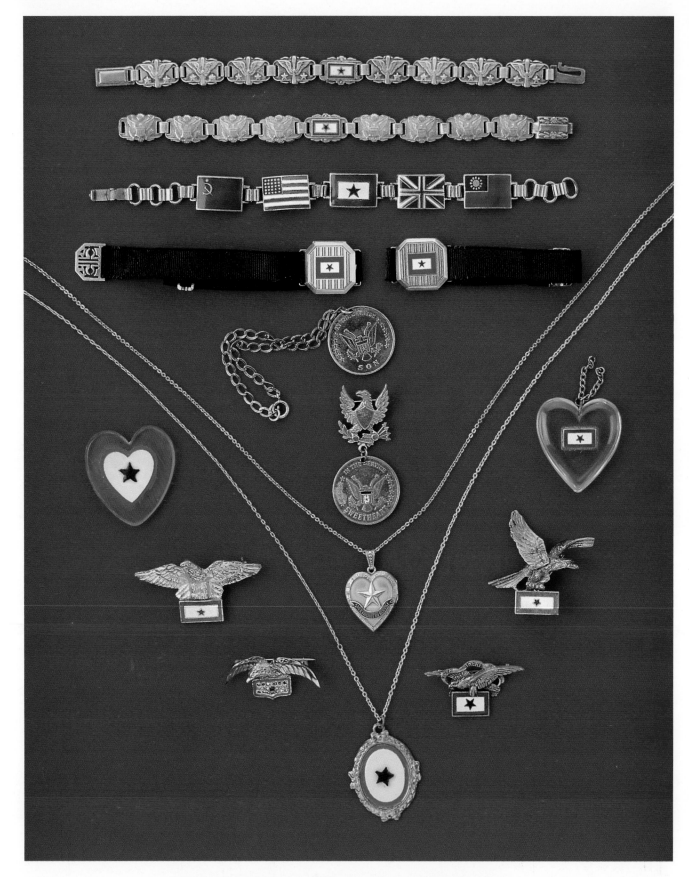

The In-service star has been in use since the beginning of World War I. The In-service jewelry shown here includes the rare and expensive forget-me-not bracelets, Allied Powers bracelets, and early cloth slide bracelets. The 14k gold slide with the black cloth band is worth several hundred dollars. The single star pins and heart pendants shown here are unique items of the In-service category. Circa 1917 to 1945.

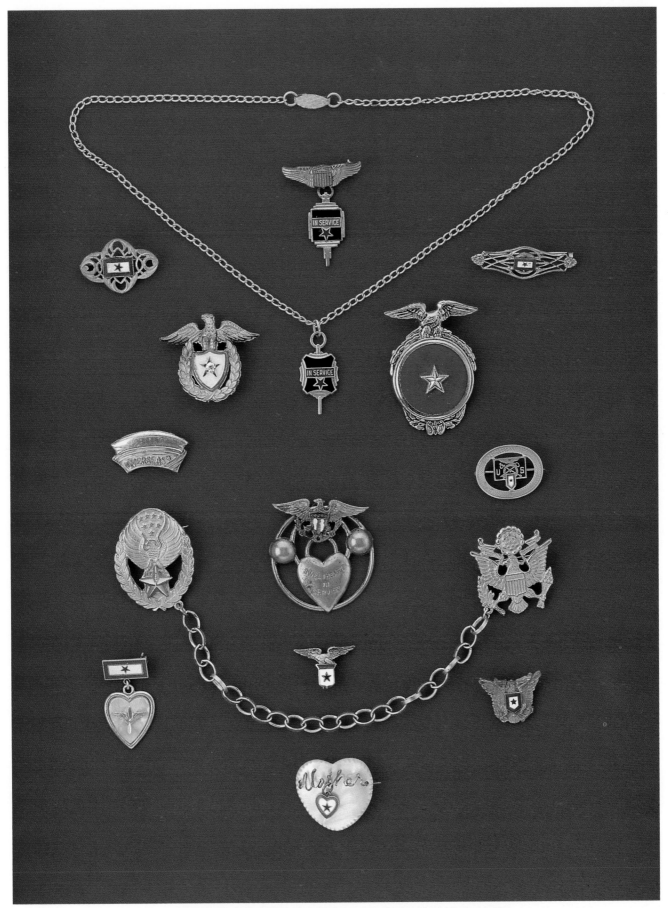

The necklace pendant has a service star. The pins in this group. Circa 1917 to 1945, are of different styles including one with two pins and a chain. The pierced oval pins at the upper right and upper left date from World War I.

In the top row the three pins represent the U. S. Navy, U. S. Army, and U. S. Marine Corps. They are all sterling silver and among the most decorative In-service pins that were made. The V (for victory) with the eagle holding the service star had a powerful meaning. The pins and pendants at the lower portion of the photograph are sterling and represent the service branches.

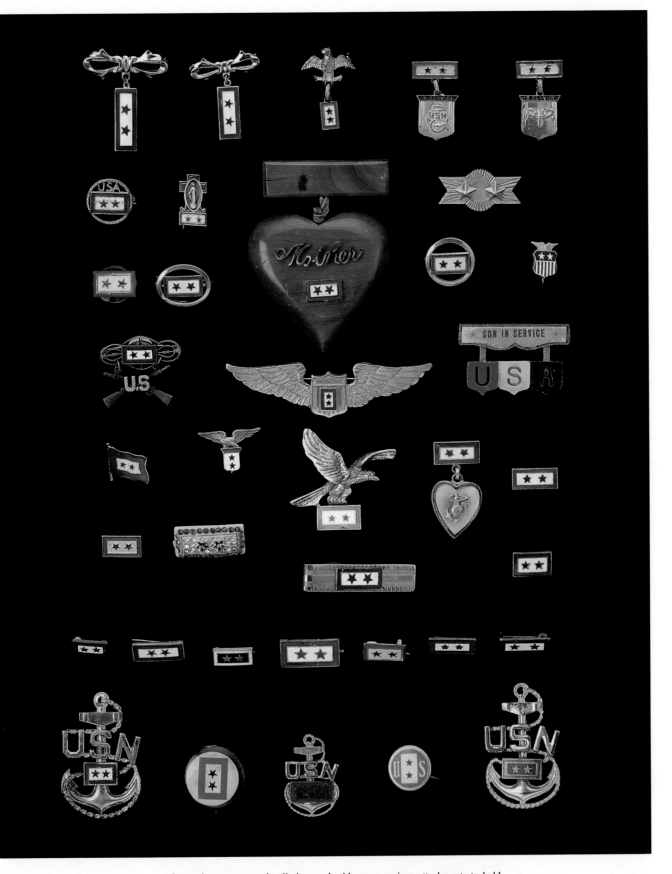

In-service stars came in all sizes and with many various attachments to hold or secure them. The different branches of service would have their own service stars. The pair of wings with two stars is very rare. The wooden homemade heart is also a rare piece. The most common In-service pin was a single bar with a blue star on a background of white, bordered in red. Circa 1917 - 1945.

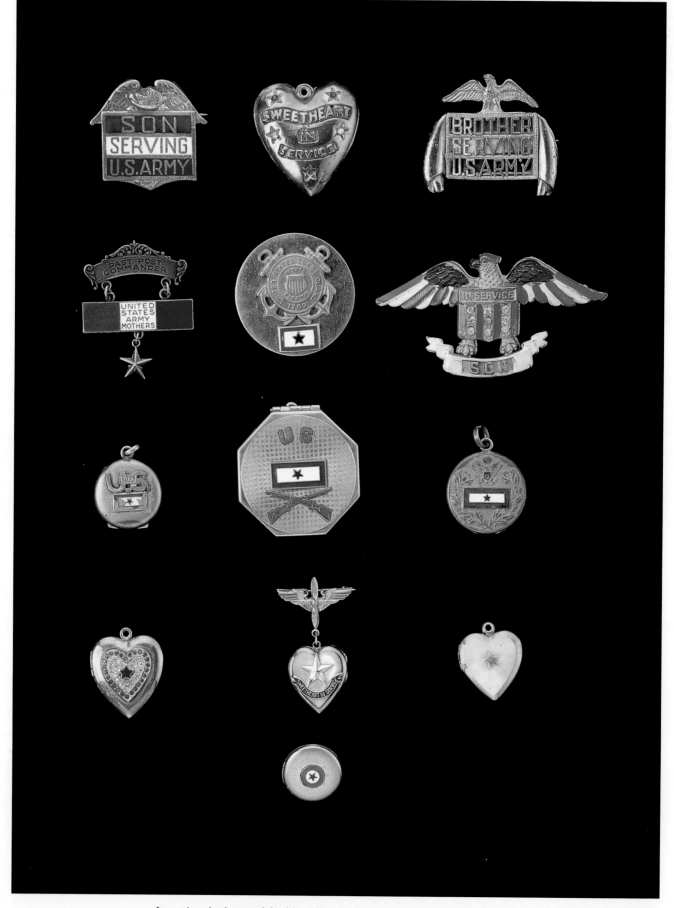

In-service pins became joined by other pin designs to convey a message
such as (at upper right) Brother in U. S. Army. A Mother pin (left in second
row) is rare. The lockets and pendants are rare. Circa 1917 - 1945.

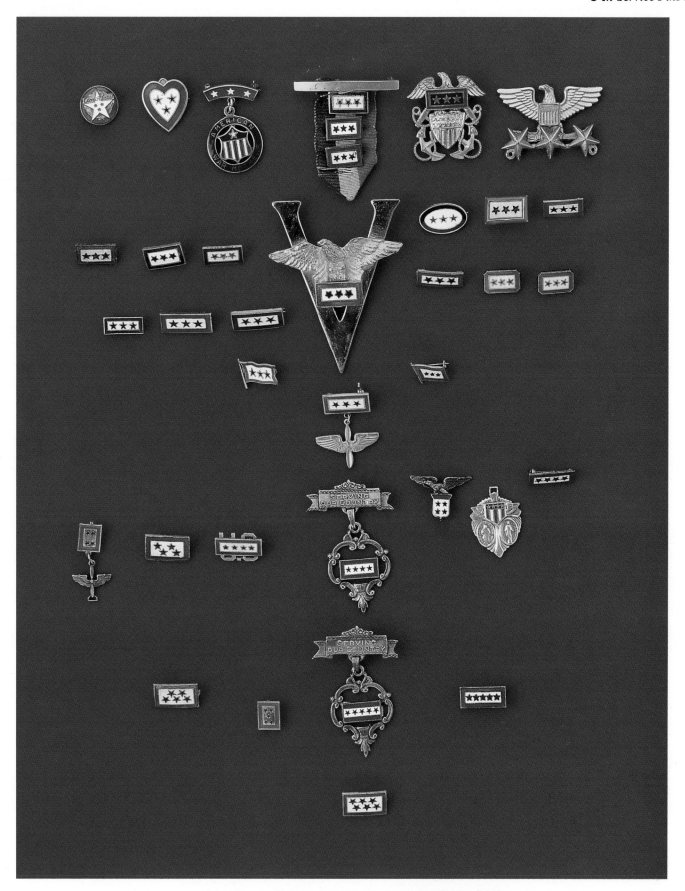

For each person in the military service, a star would adorn the pin of choice. It was very rare for a family to have more than four members in service. Pins showing five or six members (such as those pictured here) command very high prices. In this picture there are many styles of pins that ranged from three to six In-service stars.

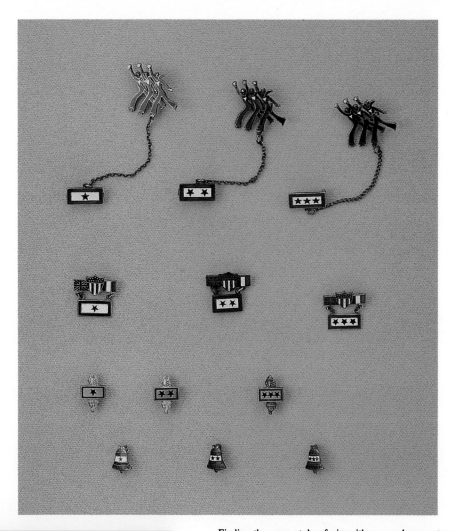

Finding the same style of pin with one and more stars is very unusual. Here are four examples of this limited group. Circa 1917 to 1945. The first row has sailors attached by a chain. The second row is from World War I and shows the flags of the Allied Powers.

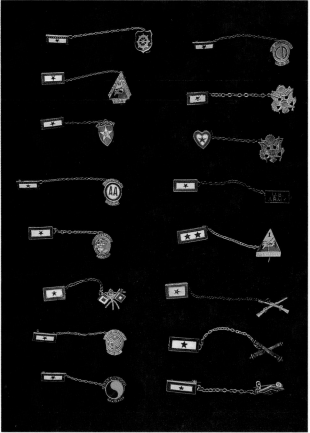

Chain pins with In-service stars attached to a military emblem were very popular. All of these represent the U. S. Army. Circa 1940 - 1945.

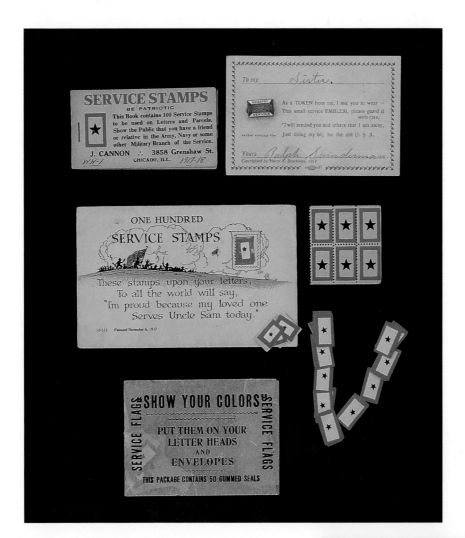

These original paper items show that In-service designations were not limited to pins. Circa 1917 to 1945.

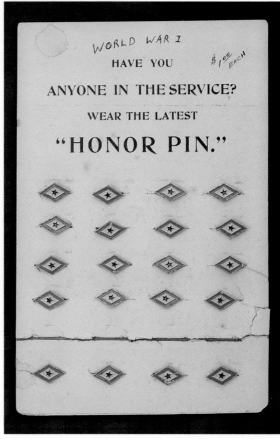

This very rare original counter top display card with the inscription "Honor Pin" is from the World War I era. It continues to fuel the controversy over calling the pins "Mother Pins," "Service Stars," "Honor Pins," or "In-service Pins."

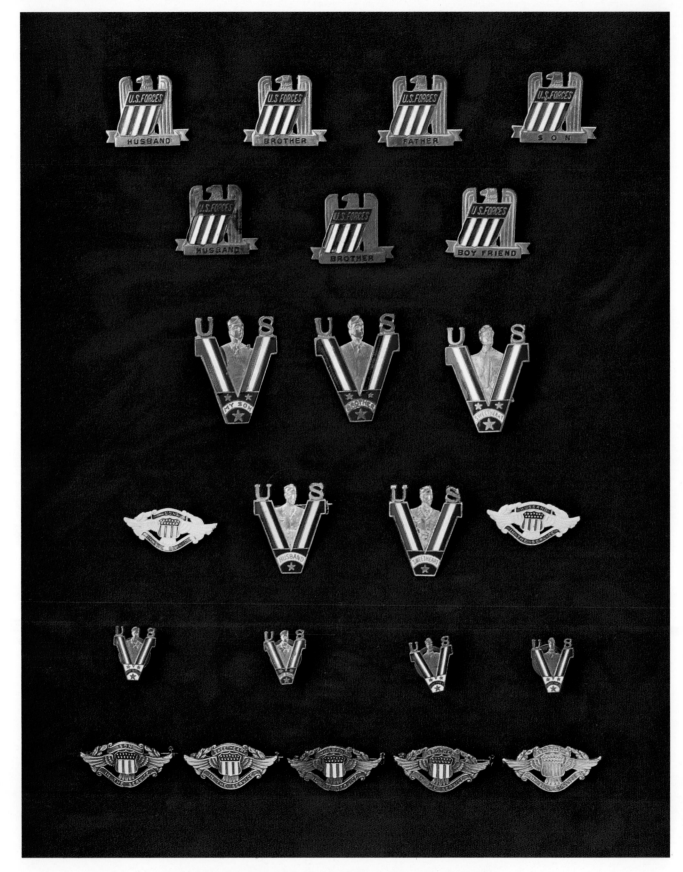

At the top, the In-service pins are in the forms of eagles with a U. S. shield and the words "Husband," "Brother," or "Son." The V-sign with a soldier outline show a relationship of "Son," "Brother," "Mother," "Sweetheart," and "Husband." The winged pins with shield also have the relationships shown. All of these were worn to display patriotism and the love of a service person. Circa 1917 - 1945.

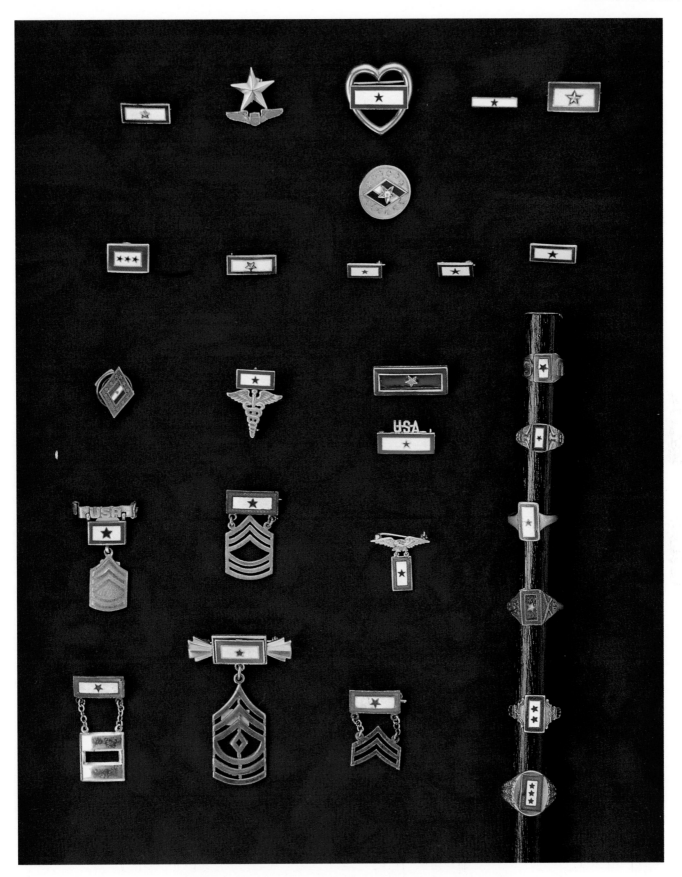

Shown are some very rare and unusual In-service pins. The pins in the first row are gold. The single pin (first row, second from left) was made by Tiffany & Co. It is one of only two Tiffany pieces in the collection of over 5,000 sweetheart jewelry items. The rank insignia In-service pins are also very uncommon. In the right column are very rare rings with from one to three In-service stars. Circa 1917 - 1945.

Picture frames were popular during World War I for In-service personnel.
The frames here retain their original pictures. The official In-service brooch
is shown attached to an original merchandising card, thereby increasing its
value. Circa, 1917 - 1919.

Here we have several examples of In-service pins attached to their original sales cards. Several are from World War I, such as the one with crossed rifles and another with "U. S." over a machine gun. Pins attached to their original card will have a higher value.

Collecting sweetheart and keepsake jewelry from other countries will usually pose a real challenge. First, there is usually a language barrier and second, there can be a lack of in-depth military knowledge. Very few sellers at the military and antique shows can offer substantial historical background. The best source for information will often be a native countryman or the good old public library.

In this section, five countries other than the United States are represented: Canada, Germany, Australia, France, and Great Britain. Articles photographed include eight bracelets representing three countries, one ring, over a dozen wing pins and five victory pins.

Items are constructed of plastic, Lucite, sterling silver, brass, gold plate, ceramic, and metal alloys and they are often enhanced with colored enamel and rhinestones. They represent both World Wars I and II.

In reviewing the items from Canada, it is interesting to note that the colors of red, white and blue appear on a victory pin as well as on In-service pins. Collectors should note that the Canadian In-service pin depicts a blue maple leaf in lieu of the star used by the United States; this is not a well-known fact. In this collection there are one-, two-, and five-maple leaf In-service pins. The five-maple leaf pin is very rare. The 20-plus items photographed were obtained while collecting at shows in Canada.

There are six German collectibles in this section and they appear all to be a product of "Trench Art" from World War I. Soldiers filled many lonely hours creating military-oriented items from products at hand. Five of the six items shown are constructed from the projectile of a bullet. The bracelet is made from a cannon casing. The data on four of these six items documents 1914 to 1918, the time period of "The Great War." World War I "Trench Art" items are rare and seldom found at military shows or auctions.

Australia is represented with six items, the most notable being the military brooch on its original card, which is a rare find in the international category.

France is the country least represented in this collection and very few items are shown. Possibly this is because of its position during the Wars and the fact that its occupation by Nazi Germany severely impacted the time it could produce military keepsake items. The French Resistance is represented by the High-Low cross. It is interesting to note the use of red, white, and blue colors on pins from France.

The United Kingdom, or Great Britain, as many referred to our English allies, has the largest number of collectibles of the five countries represented. Note the "Bundles for Britain" support pin. "Bundles for Britain" was founded in 1940 by an American socialite to provide non-military aid to the British people who were besieged by German military forces. Items such as medicine, clothing, and blankets were collected from American citizens and shipped to Britain. "There'll always be an England" was another popular slogan of the times.

Most British items pictured in this section are distinguished by the addition of rhinestones. Three pins, representing armor, artillery and victory, all have rhinestones incorporated in their design. Also, wings, which were a popular British jewelry item, are generally enhanced with colorful rhinestones. Perhaps the RAF (Royal Air Force) set the fashion standard for the Canadian and American sweetheart wings that followed later.

Other notable British features include ornate details and colorful enameling as shown on a variety of pins.

Two bracelets with the crown emblems are both "Trench Art" from World War I. To fill the lonely hours in the miles of trenches, soldiers would create items from materials at hand, such as bullet casings or scraps of metal.

Overall, collectors will find great interest, unusual beauty, a tremendous opportunity for specialization, and the chance to explore new ground in the international area.

British items from World Wars I and II are not easily found in the United States. The pins shown here are not all Sweetheart pins, some are military unit pins that could have been given to a loved one as a keepsake. The rhinestone pins with cannons and tanks are Sweetheart pins. Circa 1917 - 1945.

Bracelets from foreign countries that are made for loved ones are very hard to find in the United States. The two bracelets at the top are handmade and were created during the time of World War I. The pin on the right is made from 14k gold and is inscribed "UBIQUE." Enameled pins and glass pins were popular. Circa 1917 - 1945.

Dear Nick:

enclosed find the 2 WW1 Brit sweetheart pins we discussed.

The "horseshoe" pin H.M. Submarines was done in WW1 before the Brits' learned that by turning the shoe upside down all the luck ran out. This is one of a family of pins which I understand included many regimentals.

The "anchor" - is hallmarked, sterling and was done by the Captain of the submarine for his wife. The enlisted folks just didn't have the cash to put out for goodies like this.

Best regards,
Bill

The hand-written letter explains what these British pins are.

Australian pins are difficult to find in the United States. The pin in the center is on its original card which reads "Fashionable Military Brooch." The pin is inscribed "Australian Commonwealth Military Forces." Other pins mention service as sailors and soldiers. At the upper right is a pin inscribed "From defense for duty done," circa 1917 - 1945.

These French pins from 1917 to 1945 are among the rarest international collectibles found in the United States.

These "Trench Art" items are World War I German Sweetheart collectibles. Five are made from bullet heads and the bracelet is a very rare piece made from a cannon shell casing. Circa 1917 - 1919.

Canadian items are more frequently found in the United States than other foreign items, perhaps an indication that more were produced. The R.A.F. (Royal Air Force) wings with rhinestones are among the most sought after today, and more valuable than most of the other Canadian pieces shown. Circa 1940 - 1945.

Canadian Sweetheart jewelry and collectibles offer the same beauty and versatility as their US counterparts. Shown are Lucite hearts, Victory pins and bracelets. Note that the Canadian In-service pins have maple leaves, not stars as in the U. S. In-service pins.

LOCKETS

One of the most popular and beautiful keepsake collectibles was the locket. The locket had it all, beauty as well as usefulness by holding a picture of a loved one close to the heart.

Lockets were usually heart shaped but can also be found in round and oval shapes. Some lockets were even designed in the shape of a book.

The wearing of lockets reached its popularity peak from 1941 to 1946 and it is one collectible that is still going strong well into the Nineties.

Sizes of lockets in this collection range from one-half to two inches in length. A wire or metal hanger spelling out "sister," "mother," or "sweetheart" can add another inch in length. Lockets found in original boxes will generally command a higher price.

Lockets are most frequently made from hard cast metal with a gold or silverplate finish. They can also be found in sterling, mother-of-pearl and 10k and 14k gold.

Not all lockets will be on chains; a hanger consisting of a bald eagle or metal bow provided a decorative pin arrangement in many cases. It was also popular to have the locket hang from wire words such as "mother," "sister," or "wife."

Lockets could be purchased at the Post Exchange at nearly all military bases throughout the United States. All branches of the service have lockets with their distinctive emblem displayed on the front. The Army is represented by the American eagle. The Navy is represented by an anchor with USN inscribed through it. The Marine Corps is represented by an eagle, globe and anchor.

The Air Force will show a pair of wings with a propeller running throught it or a pair of wings with an emblem of the US shield which shows the American eagle.

The Coast Guard emblem shows crossed anchors with a shield in the center. Generally the words "The United States Coast Guard" will be written in a circle around the emblem.

Some lockets have the section of a branch of service displayed. Examples of this would be two crossed flags representing the Signal Corps, twin towers representing the Corps of Engineers, or two crossed rifles referring to the Infantry.

In this collection about one in ten lockets will have a picture in it. Most frequently the picture is of a soldier in uniform. Most lockets will have a place for two pictures. The ones that do not are usually the type that have a slide opening.

Today lockets can be located at most major collectible shows or very large flea markets. Antique dealers will also have military lockets as well as a number of other keepsake collectibles that were so popular for the home front supporters.

In collecting lockets, it is possible to hear some very interesting stories from the sellers if by chance one was an original owner. This was the case in a Webster, Florida flea market in 1993 when a woman in her early 70s revealed to the author the price of a 50-year old locket, but in the same breath said not to open the locket at this time as the picture inside was not that of her husband who sat a short distance away in a lawn chair. Must have been quite a romance!

These lockets show (left to right) the U. S. Army, Signal Corps, U. S. Infantry, and U. S. Army. Circa 1917 - 1945.

Lockets with wire hangers spelling "Sweetheart," "Mother," "Wife," or "Sister" are not common. The locket at the lower right also has the U. S. Army Transportation emblem on it. Circa 1940 - 1945.

These lockets are shaped as books and they were made to hold photographs.
Circa 1940 - 1945.

Five U. S. Army lockets are shown, At the lower left note the insignia of the
Corps of Engineers. Circa 1940 - 1945.

U. S. Army lockets including (upper left) crossed cannons which represent the Artillery Corps and (lower right) a twin towered castle which represents the Corps of Engineers. Circa 1917 - 1945.

U. S. Army lockets including (upper left) crossed flags which represent the Signal Corps. The large heart in the center measures almost 2" in length and is one of the largest lockets in this collection. Circa 1917 - 1945.

These two sterling silver lockets (shown with both fronts and backs) are very rare. The top locket for the U. S. Army has Uncle Sam on one side and clear space to inscribe a company regiment and serial number. The bottom locket for the U. S. Navy has space to inscribe the name of a ship, rate, division and ship number. The Army locket also has the word "Mizpah" which means "watchtower" and is derived from a parting salutation in Genesis xxxi 49. This type of locket was given as a gift to those who were going away, particularly departing soldiers and sailors. Uncle Sam is offering the beacon of light to servicemen. Circa 1917 - 1919.

First World War U. S. Army lockets. The upper right locket is exceptionally attractive. The very rare doughboy locket represents a guard looking after the person pictured in the locket. Circa 1917 - 1919.

U. S. Navy lockets from World War II typify the average lockets found today. Circa 1940 - 1945.

U. S. Navy lockets in sterling silver (upper left and lower right) and mother-of-pearl with the word "Sweetheart" in script. Circa 1940 - 1945.

U. S. Navy lockets with four different hanging bars: a freehand script "Sister," a script "Sister" over a mother-of-pearl bar, a script "Mother" over a goldtone bar, and a bow knot. Circa 1940 - 1945.

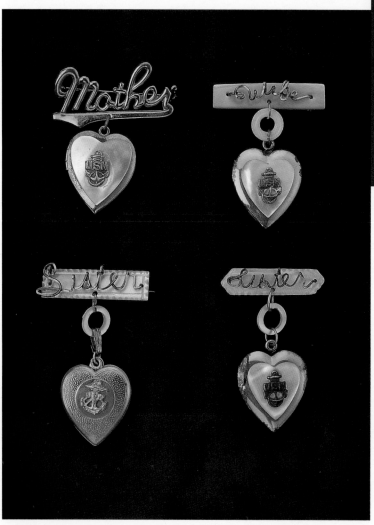

U. S. Navy lockets with the words "Mother," "Sister" or "Wife." The combination of goldtone metal, mother-of-pearl and silver makes them quite attractive. Heart shapes were very popular. Circa 1940 - 1945.

U. S. Marine Corps lockets displaying combinations of metals and words, heart and round shapes. The "Mother" locket is of especially fine quality. Of nearly 200 lockets closely inspected, fewer than ten have a manufacturer's name.

U. S. Air Force lockets include one with rhinestones (upper right). Real and simulated mother-of-pearl are featured here. Circa 1940 - 1945.

U. S. Coast Guard lockets are not common in the marketplace. The Coast Guard emblem, crossed anchors and a shield, usually has the words "United States Coast Guard" around the outer edge. The Latin phrase "Semper Paratus" (Always Ready) appears on the shield.

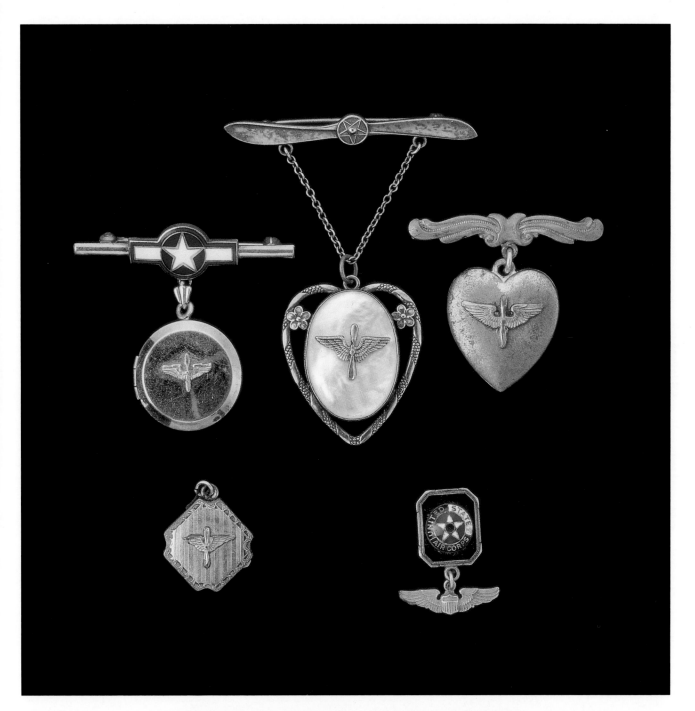

Beautiful U. S. Air Force/ Army Air Force lockets with various hangers range from ribbon to a propeller shape. The goldtone metal and mother-of-pearl background make them attractive. Circa 1940 - 1945.

U. S. Air Force/ Army Air Force lockets in mother-of-pearl and silver
depict a book design. Circa 1940 - 1945.

U. S. Air Force/ Army Air Force lockets with script "Mother" hangers and special decorations. Rhinestones and hand painted flowers distinguish these lockets as very rare and desirable. Circa 1940 - 1945.

U. S. Air Force/ Army Air Force lockets with bow knot hangers. Circa 1940 - 1945.

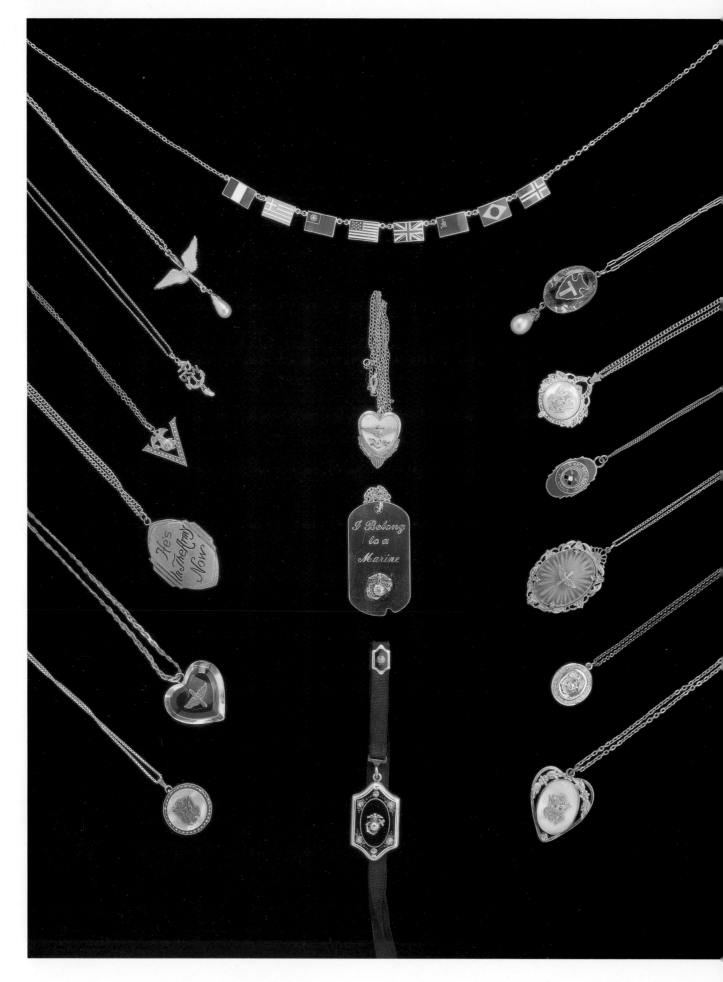

NECKLACES AND PENDANTS

Wives, sweethearts and mothers delighted in wearing necklaces and pendants that showed support for a loved one involved in the war effort. What a beautiful way to show pride and patriotism so close to the heart!

A number of the pendants shown in this chapter are lockets and have pictures of soldiers inside. Pendants without chains are shown in the pin section of this book.

Most necklaces and pendants represent a branch of the service. Of the 130 items in this collection, thirty-nine have an Army affiliation, twenty-two are Navy, forty-two are Air Force, and ten are Marine Corps. There are also pendants representing the US Army Air Force and the American Expeditionary Force from World War I. Some pendants express sentiments such as "He's in the Army Now," or "All my love always." One colorful necklace depicts the flags of the Allied powers.

Many of the Navy necklaces and pendants in this section show an anchor with the initials "USN." The Army is represented by an American eagle. The Marine Corps will show an eagle, globe and anchor. The Coast Guard emblem depicts crossed anchors with a shield in the center and usually the words "United States Coast Guard" will surround the emblem. The Air Force will show a pair of wings with an emblem of the US shield which shows the American eagle or wings with a propeller blade.

Collectors will find enormous variety in this area of sweetheart jewelry. Pendants were fashioned in the shape of hearts, books, dog tags, torpedoes, bullets and military insignias. They can be circular, rectangular or oval. Several pendants feature a pearl that drops from a semi-precious stone or a pilot's wing.

In the marketplace pendants can be found in a variety of colors such as jade green, gold, silver, blue enamel, chrome, brass, garnet, ruby, sapphire blue, and combinations of blue and black and also red, white and blue.

Pendants were created from sterling silver, glass, Lucite, semi-precious stones, bullets, 14k and 10k gold, gold and silver plate, scrap metal, brass and mother-of-pearl. Some were handcrafted from buttons, coins and military insignias mounted on wooden circles.

Of interest to collectors are the examples of "Pacific War Art" that are depicted on at least nine articles. The pendant made from an Australian coin and the carved Lucite hearts are all considered "Pacific War Art." This was jewelry that was handcrafted by soldiers during the lonely hours of World War II. They used materials at hand, such as the Lucite from windshields of downed aircraft.

In this collection there are two sets of jewelry items with identical emblems. One is a set consisting of a bracelet and necklace, and the other set is a necklace and a pin. These are rare finds in the marketplace. Also of interest is the fact that many pendants were made plain to allow jewelers or the serviceman himself to create a personal piece of sweetheart jewelry.

The hangers of the pendants are as interesting as the pendants themselves. In this collection, there are hangers made from handcrafted plastic links, velveteen cord, a G.I. shoestring, forget-me-not links, large costume jewelry links, ribbon and, of course, the most popular choices -- gold or sterling silver chains.

Manufacturers of these pendants include Brantel, N.Y.C.; Uris Sales Corp., N.Y.C.; Coro, Crest Craft and Theda, just to name a few.

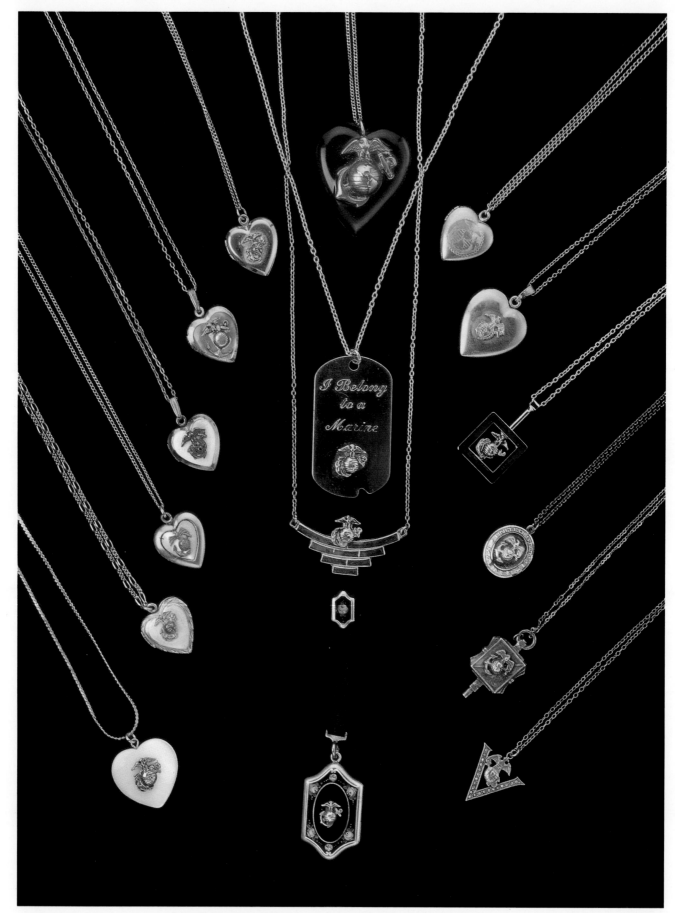

U. S. Marine Corps pendants and necklaces which range from those of moderate value (Lucite heart) to high value (black sterling silver slide on cloth roping at the center). Circa 1940.

U. S. Navy necklaces and pendants. The 14k gold pendant with a pearl drop at the bottom center dates from the First World War era and is very rare. The Lucite heart was quite possibly made from the windshield of a downed fighter aircraft. The amethyst pendant is mounted with an officers' insignia. Circa 1917 to 1945.

U. S. Navy and Coast Guard pendants and necklaces of various styles including the novelty "P"-coat button and a dog tag shape that reads "I belong to a sailor." Others show a ship, torpedo or anchor. Circa 1917 - 1945.

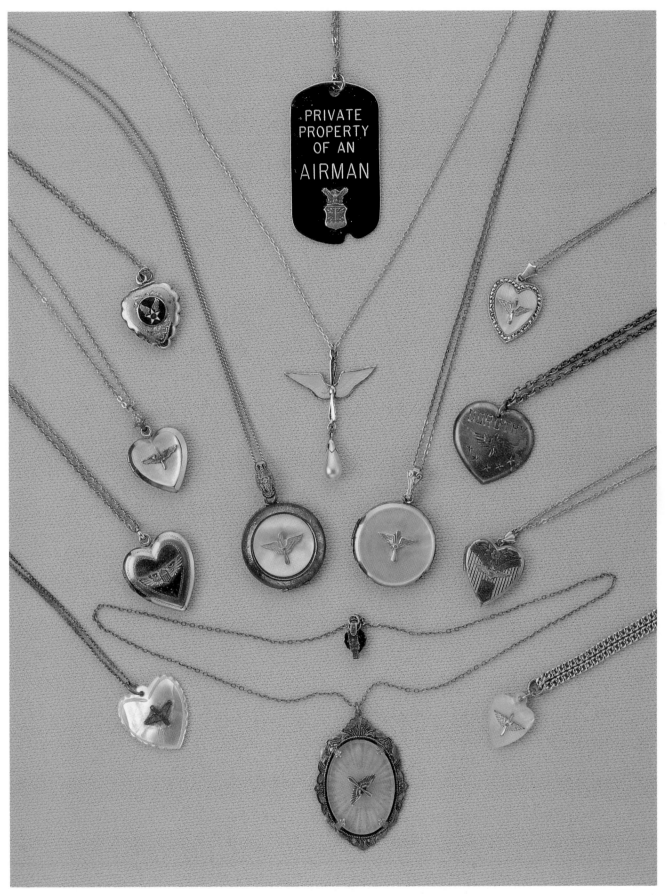

Army Air Force/ U. S. Air Force pendants. The dog tag style pendant reads
"Private Property of an Airman." The golden wings with a pearl drop is
very rare. Other materials include mother-of-pearl, glass, sterling silver and
gold. Circa 1917 - 1945.

Army Air Force/ U. S. Air Force Lucite heart pendants shown are handmade
with wings or airplane emblems. The bottom left chain is made of plastic.
The top center heart, inscribed "Army, Helen 1943 - 1944," is a wonderful
example of Pacific War Art. Circa 1940 - 1945.

The pendant second from the top is inscribed "He's in the Army Now" and
the reverse side is inscribed "U. S. Army." The third necklace is made from
army buttons attached to wood. The forget-me-not necklace with an In-
service star is sterling silver. The bottom necklace shows the flags of the
Allied Forces in sterling silver. Circa 1940 - 1945.

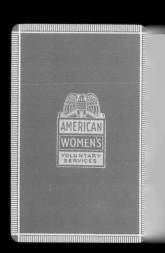

PLAYING CARDS

"Who cares for you?" said Alice...You're nothing but a pack of playing cards!" --Lewis Carroll, *Alice's Adventures in Wonderland.*

Playing cards was a source of mental and social recreation to thousands of servicemen world-wide. A good card game helped soldiers on the front line while away the hours of waiting in the trenches, in the field hospitals, in the Red Cross and USO facilities, on board ships, trains and planes.

Cards had the merits of being small, neat, inexpensive, and very social.

In the marketplace it is difficult to find complete decks of cards. Many cards either got worn out or thrown out. Single cards can be purchased usually for about $1.00, while a complete single deck is in the $25.00 range.

Prominent designs found on military cards include the eagle followed by "V" for victory showing military rank insignia up and down the "V".

"Bundles for America" and "Let's hit back hard" were other popular themes during the war years, along with Uncle Sam, Miss Liberty, and pictures of battleships and airplanes.

Cartoon characters frequently were featured on the faces of cards, sometimes showing the enemy in undignified positions.

Of great interest to collectors are the cards used for educational purposes. The Naval Aviation training division produced a flash deck of US Navy and International Code Flag cards. It featured numeral and special pennants, international code flags, special flags and morse code symbols.

In 1943, Burton Crane issued a French lingo pack to help American servicemen learn French. It has 108 cards with five phrases on each card.

"Convoy," as pictured in this chapter, was an identification game made in England that familiarized civilians with combat and auxiliary ships of the US Navy.

Also in the educational category, aircraft recognition silhouette cards were produced by the U.S. Playing Card Company of Cincinnati, Ohio. These spotter playing cards helped soldiers and civilians learn the characteristics of United Nations and enemy aircraft. The Lockheed P-38, Zero, Spitfire and Messerschmitt characteristics were all identified along with many other types of aircraft.

The variety of cards in the marketplace will never cease to amaze the collector. Some cards feature branches of the service such as the medical, armored, cavalry or field artillery corps. Other cards designate a military base such as Camp Crowder, Missouri. Patriotic decks of cards were also distributed by companies to their employees to promote efficiency as well as patriotism.

In this collection there is a set of two Grumman aviation decks in the original box. One deck, still in cellophane with the Internal Revenue stamp affixed, features the Grumman "Hellcat" aircraft. The opened deck features the Grumman "Avenger."

World War II cards are represented by a deck that shows British Field Marshall Montgomery surrounded by tanks. This deck was manufactured by Universal Playing Card Company, LTD, of Crown Point, NORICS Leeds.

Also featured in this chapter is a double deck of Martin aircraft cards in original cellophane with the Internal Revenue stamp affixed. The decks show the US Navy P5 M-1 and the P5 M-2 planes, both amphibious aircraft of this era. This set was manufactured by Brown, Bigelow, of St. Paul, Minnesota.

World War I playing cards generally feature pictures of heads of state, noteworthy generals, and action scenes from Triple Alliance or Allied countries. German packs displayed the Kaiser and *Hindenberg* and *Tirpitz*. The Montreal Lithograph Company produced a pack which showed kings and generals and private soldiers of the Allied Forces and had six national flags on the backs.

World War II playing cards repeated many of the patterns of the First World War. In 1943, Biermans of Turnhour, Belgium, issued a Jeep pack in anticipation of liberation. It has Jeeps on the back, and on the aces are the heads of Stalin, Montgomery, Eisenhower and de Gaulle. The Universal Playing Card Company, previously known as Alf Cooke & Co., published a Victory pack in 1944 which had portraits of Allied leaders, including Roosevelt and Stalin, on the backs over the motto "United We Stand;" and in the very same year Belgium issued a pack with the motto "Union Fait La Force" and pictures of the Allied leaders. Churchill was drawn as the king of spades, Roosevelt as the king of diamonds, Stalin as the king of hearts, and de Gaulle as king of clubs. Hitler takes the part of a joker and is shown with a bomb dropping on his head. In 1941, the E.E. Fairchild Corporation, of Rochester, New York, printed a "Bundles for Britain" pack with a golden lion and shield on the back, below which appeared the initials "B.W.R.S."

These patriotic playing cards helped build morale with their red, white and
blue colors and eagle designs. The set at the lower left shows U. S. Naval
officer's emblems. Circa 1940 - 1945.

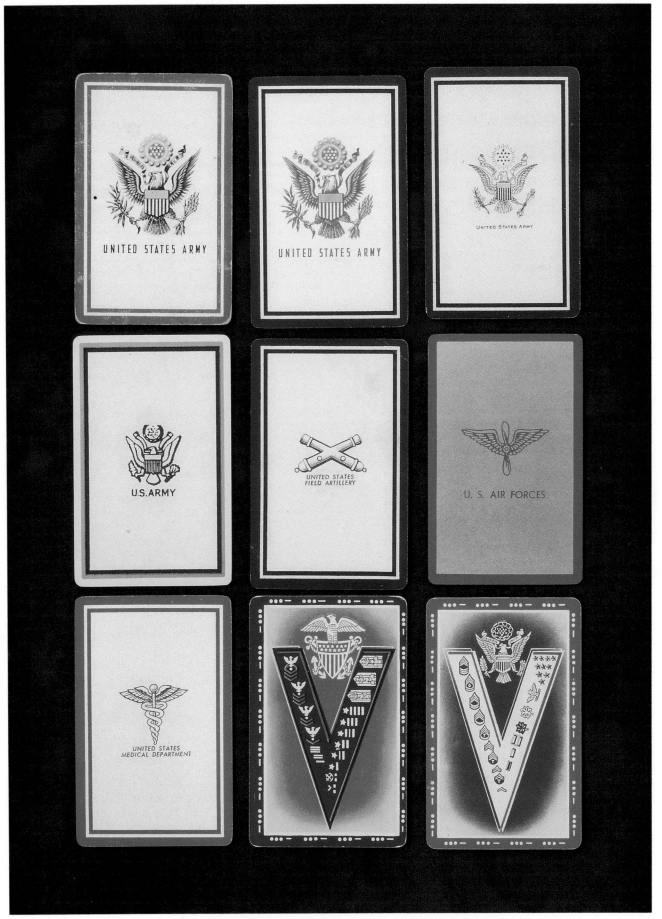

Sets of playing card showing different branches of the service and a large V
for victory. Circa 1940 - 1945.

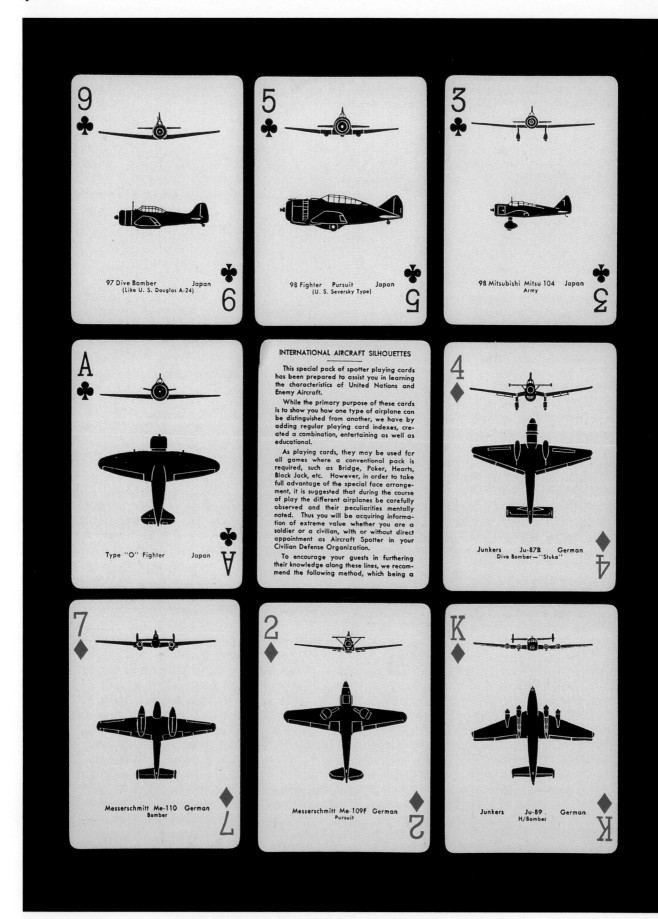

This "Spotter deck" of playing cards had silhouettes of international enemy aircraft. They were used to educate the public as a precaution against attack. Circa 1942 - 1945.

POSTCARDS

American military postcards, with their strong emphasis on humor, will always be a sought after Home Front collectible. It is hard to believe that military life could be presented in so many humorous ways. The motto for illustrators must truly have been "Let's keep them laughing."

Comic postcards were very colorful and were a popular souvenir from various military camps, such as a set published for Camp Davis, Holly Ridge, North Carolina. Subjects such as hiking, ill-fitting uniforms, laundry, chow, and dishwashing were humorously presented for the sake of keeping morale high.

Postcards collected from the 1940s are "linens" which feature a textured linen-like paper surface. They frequently were sold in sets of ten for the price of ten cents. A one-cent stamp was required for mailing each card in the United States and a two-cents stamp for mailing to a foreign country.

Folding postcards were sold to soldiers to send home to their families. They could help explain to loved ones back home their military training by showing pictures of equipment, training exercises, barracks, mess hall and the church.

In the marketplace, collectors will find propaganda postcards that were mass-produced to encourage patriotism. Hitler was a favorite figure that was posed in many undignified situations. It is not uncommon to see postcards flushing Mine Fuehrer down the toilet, getting a swift "kick" from U.S. soldiers, or being crushed in some fashion by his own *Mein Kampf* book.

In contrast to the humorous American postcards, the Germans presented serious subject matter such as armed forces personnel in action.

Whatever the subject matter, collecting military postcards is a delightful way to specialize in a vast area of collectibles whose origin can be traced back to a pre-1898 era.

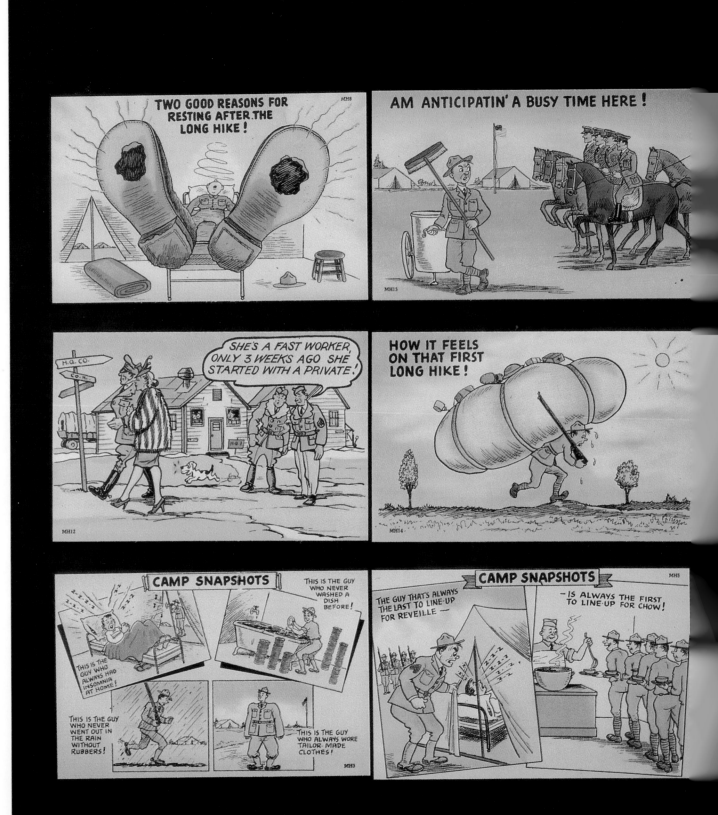

Post cards with humorous themes directed at the daily routines of service personnel were very popular. For example, the center right card shows a soldier carrying a pack nearly three times larger than he is. Circa 1940 - 1945.

Black and white post cards were popular during World War II to relate humorous situations of duty and create a smile during a worrisome era. Circa 1940 - 1945.

RATION BOOKS

"If you don't need it, don't buy it."

Ration books were used to enable governments to control the allocation of resources and to ensure that scarce materials were devoted to the war effort.

For a people almost totally unused to any kind of wartime sacrifice, War Production Board Directive No. 1 to the Office of Price Administration, January, 1942 -instituting rationing- came as a shock. Suddenly, U.S. citizens were stuck with a mess of little books and stamps that limited the food or gas they could buy. What's more, the instructions on how to use the food stamps seemed incomprehensible (boxed at right).

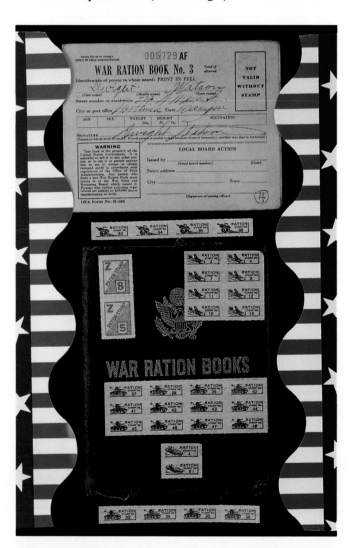

Ration cards and stamps were a part of everyday life from 1942 - 1945. Rationing was regulated by the Office of Price Administration of the US Government.

Rationing hit home in the kitchen, in the workplace, and on the road. As many as three billion ration coupons, the nations's second currency, changed hands each month.

In the summer of 1942, even before it was rationed, gasoline was already scarce along the East Coast. The military got what it needed first. By year's end, Roosevelt imposed a 35 mph national speed limit.

No more new homes would be built. No more commercial trucks. Production of civilian radios, refrigerators, washing machines and other appliances was banned for the duration. The War Production Board even outlawed trouser cuffs---to save on fabric.

Because of military needs for silk and nylon, women's stockings became a treasured commodity. Many American women simply began wearing slacks. Some even painted "seams" on their legs.

To those who complained about shortages or shoddy substitute goods, sales clerks had a stock reply: "Don't you know there's a war on?"

All RED and BLUE stamps in War Ration Book 4 are WORTH 10 POINTS EACH. RED and BLUE TOKENS are WORTH 1 POINT EACH. RED and BLUE TOKENS are used to make CHANGE for RED and BLUE stamps only when purchase is made. IMPORTANT! POINT VALUES of BROWN and GREEN STAMPS are NOT changed.

V-MAIL

V-Mail was a combination sheet and envelope for rush photographic mail to our Armed Forces overseas. It provided the most expeditious dispatch of messages and reduced the weight of mail to and from servicemen outside the continental United States. When addressed to points where micro-film equipment was operated, a miniature photographic negative of the message was made and sent by transportation available for reproduction and delivery. The original message was destroyed after the reproduction had been delivered. Messages addressed to or from points where micro-film equipment was not operating were transmitted in their original form by the most expeditious means available. V-Mail letters were sent free of postage by members of the Armed Forces. When sent by others, the postage was 3 cents for ordinary mail or six cents for air mail.

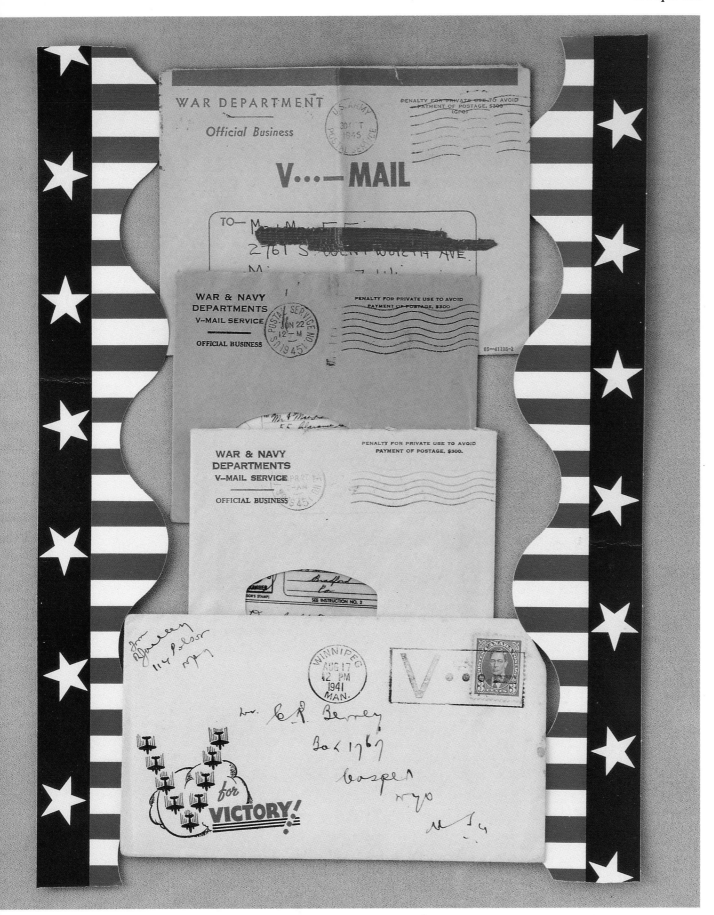

V-Mail was a combination sheet and envelope for rush photographic mail
to our Armed Forces overseas. It provided the most expeditious dispatch of
messages and reduced the weight of mail to and from service men overseas.

When collecting in the area of playing cards, greeting cards, ration cards and postcards, consider other Home Front articles such as recipes and wartime cookbooks, military manuals, handbooks for wives and mothers, blotters distributed by companies, posters, and the whole field of military stationery. It is possible to specialize in patriotic envelopes alone. The colorful wartime envelopes in the marketplace depict patriotism with slogans such as "Let's Go USA," "All Out For Victory," "Remember Pearl Harbor," and "Time For Us To Clean Up," just to name a few.

Envelopes were issued with patriotic themes, messages about Victory and working to preserve Freedom, and pictures of enemy leaders being stamped out. To instill a spirit of dedication to America, messages touching on the American historic past and heros and the glorious future would travel through the mail for the carriers to see. Circa 1940 - 1945.

These envelopes display pictures of the American flag or Uncle Sam with enthusiastic messages of working toward Victory. Circa 1940 - 1945.

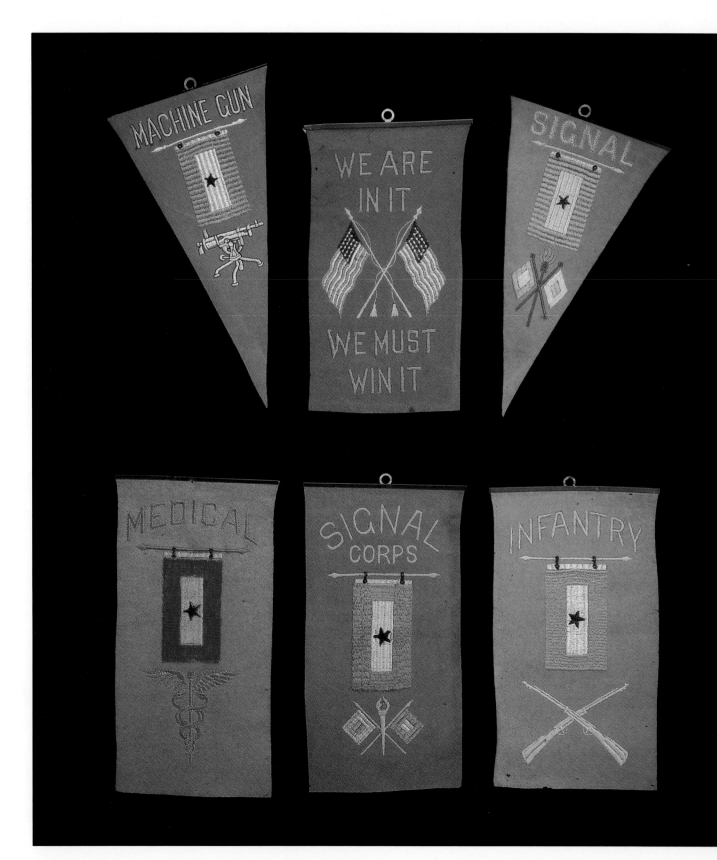

PENNANTS, BANNERS, AND FLAGS

This is an interesting area of military collectibles. Pennants, banners and flags were the largest patriotic items a family might display in their "victory" home. Usually they would be hung at the front door or in a front window to show the world a loved one was involved in the war effort.

Many pennants had an In-service emblem, which was a flag with a blue star in the center. Pennants pictured in this chapter are made of felt and have military identification embroidered on them such as the word "Infantry" with crossed rifles below, or the words "Signal Corps" with two crossed flags and a torch in the middle. There are also examples of "Medical" and "Machine Gun" pennants with the appropriate emblems. Today, this type of pennant can reach a price of $100.

Flags can represent a country, branches of the service, a unit within a branch of the service, an In-service situation, or a serviceman's rank, such as a flag with a General's star.

Of great interest to collectors are the In-service flags which were red, white and blue. They usually had a red border, white background and a blue star in the center for each person from a particular residence in the service. There are flags in the marketplace with four stars, but more than four stars would be very rare.

If a gold star appeared on a flag, as pictured in this chapter, it would mean a person had died in service. Companies would fly a flag with stars on it to show the number of employees serving in the military. These are very hard to locate today.

Banners are rectangular in shape, usually made of silk, and may denote a country. In this chapter there is a victory banner pictured showing the Allied nations of China, Great Britain, Russia and the United States. Banners also may denote a particular branch of the service or individual unit such as the Signal Corps, Medical Corps, or Infantry.

Souvenir banners with a soldier's name and military camp were popular, such as the Camp Stewart, Georgia banner that is pictured on page 109. A "welcome home" banner for the returning soldier was also a popular display of patriotism. It would usually show an eagle over crossed flags framed by a "V."

In-service banners, with a star for each family member in the service, were highly visible displays of patriotism.

Most banners in the marketplace will be from World War II. Banners from World War I are rare and not always in the best condition. They frequently were made of wool and the moths had their own war without the benefit of a peace treaty. In this collection the only World War I banner photographed says "World War Veteran" at the bottom.

Unit flags, personal flags, special event flags, and flags from Germany and Japan continue to be popular in the marketplace and always are a great source of joy for the specialized military collector.

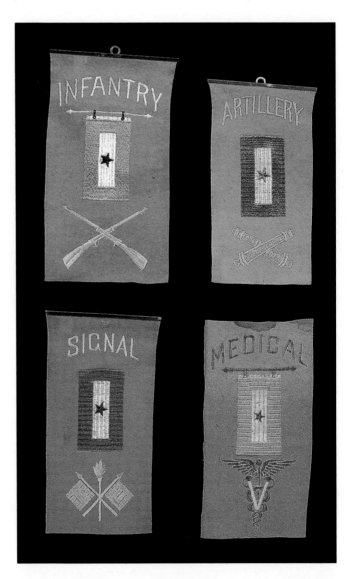

In-service pennants and banners first appeared in 1917 at the start of World War I. They were hung in windows, on walls, or from doors with designs to show the type of service the soldier was in. The crossed rifles indicates Infantry, crossed flags the Signal Corps, crossed cannon the Artillery, a twin tower castle the Engineer Corps, key-sword-wheel-eagle the Transportation Corps, eagle alone the Army, and V for Victory. Today these are very rare. Circa 1917 -1919.

The In-service flags of red, white, and blue came back into use in World War II to tell the world someone was in the service. The number of stars in the flag indicated how many people from that house were in the military. Circa 1940 - 1945.

Here examples of types of flags showing one, two, and four stars. The four star In-service flag is exceptional.

Besides the colors of red, white and blue, other insignia were used on banners and flags. The golden eagle indicates someone who has served the country and has been discharged. The blue banner indicates someone serving at Camp Stewart, Georgia. The small In-service picture frame shows one star. The Allied Nations banner shows the flags of the U. S., Russia, Great Britain and China. These flags were a visible way civilians could demonstrate their own patriotism. Circa 1917 - 1945.

PILLOW COVERS

During World War II, one of the most popular souvenirs sold to the troops were fancy satin pillow covers. Pillow covers are probably one of the most "colorful" areas a collector could specialize in. It is not uncommon to find neon pinks, red, white and blue combinations, purple, yellow, black and gold pillows framed by two-inch contrasting fringe.

Pillow covers were easy to mail home to wives, mothers and dads, sweethearts, grandmothers and sisters. They held a place of honor on Home Front couches and beds throughout the U.S..

Most of the sentimental covers had a verse of poetry, very typical of the early 1940s. Many covers featured a patriotic or location motif. Patriotic covers usually stressed a specific branch of the service or a unit. Location pillow covers either related to a specific military base, or a large city or country.

Souvenir pillow covers are generally about 22 inches square, including fringe. Most covers available are World War II vintage. Some are constructed of raised felt and some are monogrammed or hand embroidered, adding to their value.

World War I pillow covers are difficult to find. Very few have survived. In this collection, a World War I example features the American flag and the verse "For the Flag and You."

In the marketplace today, most pillow covers are in the $5 to $50 range but can go as high as $60 for a China/Burma/India cover embroidered with silver threads. Uniqueness, condition and availability are all factors in determining value.

To My Wife

A darling little wife
Has made my dreams come true
She blesses all my life
Her name is only "You."

You are my partner sweet,
You share in all I do,
And make my joy complete
By simply being You!

Mother & Dad

The voice of parents is the voice of gods
for to their children
they are heavens lieutenants.
                    -Shakespeare

Mother

M - is for the million things she gave me
O - means only that she's growing old
T - is for the tears she shed to save me
H - is for the heart of purest gold
E - is for her eyes with lovelight shining
R - means right and right she'll always be
        Put them all together
        They spell mother
        A word that means
        The world to me.

Sister

Nice to chat with, good to know,
Glad to have her where I go.
Kind in trouble, bright in joy,
Suits exactly -- can't say why.
Sweet and lonesome, always true,
That's my sister, yes, that's you.

To Grandmother

Love sends a message to grandmother dear
"May all that is happy and full of good cheer
Brighten your days year after year."

Remembering

As days pass by I never feel blue,
I remember the happy times with you.
It would lighten my cares, and double my joys
To know that you're remembering too.

Sweetheart

I thought that you would like to know
That someone's thoughts go where you go.
That someone never can forget
The hours we spent since first we met.
That life is richer sweeter for.
For such a sweetheart as you are.
And now my constant prayer will be
That God may keep you safe for me.

Pillow covers on right are World War I. These covers conveyed messages and verses of love and patriotism. Many were handmade.

Pillow covers are the most colorful of military collectibles and had a place of honor on couches and beds at the home front.

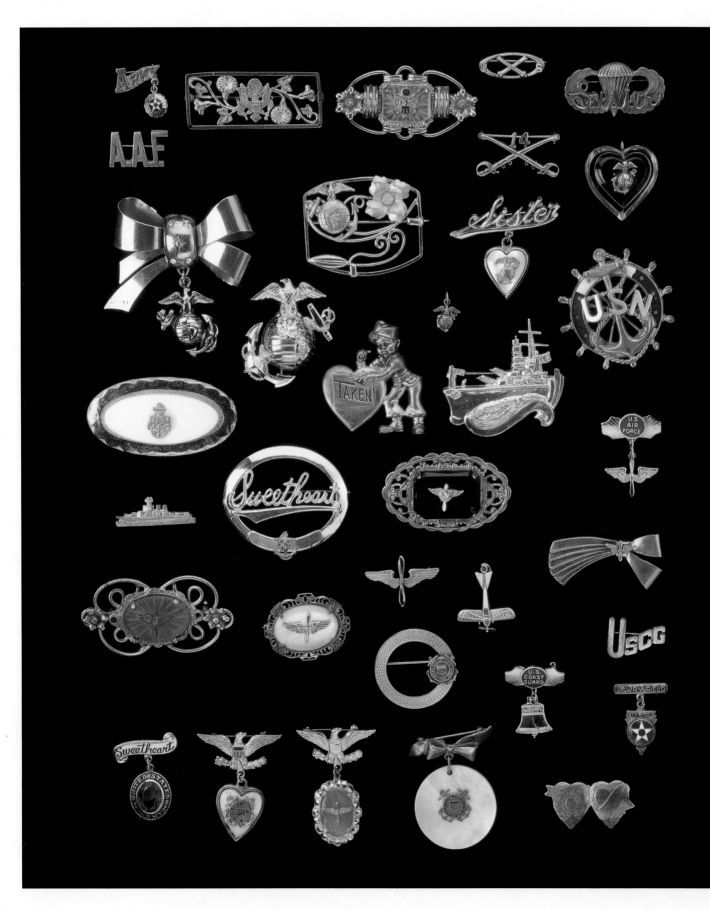

PINS

The extravagant femininity of women's fashions in the 1940s brought thousands of unusual and decorative military sweetheart items into the marketplace. Many of these items do not fall into a specialized category other than branch of service. This chapter will show nearly a 1,000 collectibles gathered over a ten year period. The fifteen display cases of items photographed show the tremendous broad base of subject matter and styles available to collectors. Throughout this chapter there will be representation from World War I to the present.

It is possible to specialize in one branch of the service or collect items from all the services as this author has chosen to do.

This chapter shows the uniqueness, beauty, and sometimes utter whimsy of pins, lockets, pendants, medals, miniature picture frames, coins, spoons, medallions, mirrors, charm bracelet pieces, hair accessories and uniform emblems, just to name a few. Although not approved by the branches of the service, some actual uniform emblems were worn by wives and sweethearts.

Subject matter of this vast category of collectibles includes individual rank insignias for the Infantry, Medical, Armor, Artillery, Signal and other units within the branches of service. Additional military designations show crossed rifles, sabres, swords, soldiers, jeeps, tanks, parachutes, anchors, wings, shields, flags, and stars.

These sweetheart items were made of glass, cloth, wood, Lucite, plastic, 14k and 10k gold, silver and gold metal alloys, sterling silver, mother-of-pearl, aluminum, tin, and rhinestone and metal combinations. Most items were manufactured but there are a few examples shown of "Trench Art "and "Pacific War Art."

The brass ordnance insignia molded into the shape of a bomb in the Army section depicts "Trench Art." A Lucite heart with a hanger in the Air Force section is a good example of "Pacific War Art." Military personnel overseas would fill up lonely hours making jewelry to send a message of love to someone back home. They would pound, carve, mold, hammer and polish any available piece of metal, wood or plastic into a piece of jewelry or momento.

The acquisition of a World War I keepsake item will add depth and excitement to any military jewelry collection. A factor that will help document a World War I piece is the non-locking back on a pin. An open latch, without benefit of a moveable cover, generally will designate a World War I time frame. This is true of a small, sterling silver heart photographed in this section. On the heart are the words "The Lord watch between me and thee when we are absent from one another."

This section has a lot to comprehend. For the sake of organization, it is necessary to take a look at each branch of the service separately.

The Navy will be generally represented by an anchor, or the initials "USN," or a combination of both. The officer's insignia is an eagle resting on a shield of crossed anchors. Navy items in this chapter frequently show rank insignia and novelty subject matter such as sabres, torpedoes and ships.

The Marine Corps will be represented by an eagle over a globe and anchor. The motto of the corps is "Semper Fidelis" (Always Faithful) and the official colors of the Corps are scarlet and gold. This chapter shows the Marine Corps emblem in fifteen different varieties of pins and pendant hangers. The emblems shown are constructed of plastic, heavy brass with rhinestones, red, white and blue enamel over metal and mother-of-pearl. One emblem is an attachment hanging from the word "Mother" written in script. It is mounted on its original card with the printed verse:

"To the best and bravest mother,
The truest friend I know,
Take this little gift,
Love and blesssings with it go."

The Air Force shows a pair of wings with a single propeller blade or just wings by themselves. The Air Force is the youngest branch of the U.S. armed forces. Until it became an independent branch in 1947, it had been part of the Army . Hence, collectors will find Army Air Corps items in the market place. One of the Army Air Corps most distinguished alums was none other than Clark Gable who flew on several bombing missions over Germany shooting footage for an aerial gunner film. He was awarded the Distinguished Flying Cross before being discharged in 1944 by Captain Ronald Reagan.

There are countless ways manufacturers have incorporated wings into jewelry. Wings may show an insignia, a number such as the 8th or 9th Air Force, a propeller, a star or a shield designating specialties and qualifications of aircraft crews, such as pilot, navigator, flight surgeon, aircrew member and so on. In this section, note the fashionable "hand" holding a heart that has an Air Force wing in the center. There is also a sterling silver hair barrette with the Air Force emblem.

The Army is recognized by a stand alone eagle. The words US Army may be written below it. The insignia worn on officer's caps is patterned after the United States coat of arms. Further subdivision by branches of the service include twin towers for the Corps of Engineers, crossed rifles for Infantry, and crossed flags for the Signal Corps. The Army motto is "This We'll Defend." The official Army flag colors are blue, white and red, with yellow fringes.

There are many different styles of Army sweetheart pins. Pins were designed as hearts to clearly signify "love," or could have the design of a four-leaf clover to convey "good luck." The use of weapons including swords, tanks, cannons, and rifles were used to send a message of defense.

Novelty pins would also send a unique message of well-intended love. An example of this is the large, gold question mark pictured in this chapter. It has the words "Who do I love?" across the arch of the pin with an arrow aimed at the period. The word "See" is on the period. When opened this small locket area exposes a picture of a soldier in combat uniform standing in front of an Army truck.

A vast majority of Army sweetheart pins will show an eagle. In the more rare category will be pins that depict parachutes or paratroopers jump wings. These pins will command a higher value than an Engineering Corps or Signal Corps pin. This is partially due to the accomplishments of being an airborne fighter, occasionally argued, in some circles, to be harder to achieve than a basic ground combatant.

The sheer number of Army sweetheart pins available in the marketplace probably stems from the fact that the Army is the oldest and largest branch of the nation's armed services. Its traditions date back to 1775, when the Continental Congress created the Continental Army. It is very feasible in this service, for a collector to specialize . Perhaps the focus would be all cavalry items that would show crossed swords, or perhaps all heart-shaped items with an Army insignia.

The Coast Guard is represented by an emblem that shows crossed anchors with a shield in the center. Generally, the words "United States Coast Guard" will be written in a circle around the emblem. The Coast Guard motto is "Semper Paratus,"(Always Ready). World War II saw the Coast Guard serving as a specialized branch of the Navy.

Coast Guard pins are not common in the market place. There are less than 30 shown in this section and less than 50 shown in this total book of almost 3,000 collectibles. This service seldom got the big headlines, but nevertheless had a big challenge on its hands. It was asked to protect a coast line that measured over 3,000 miles. During WW II, the Coast Guard took part in Pacific operations and developed beach-landing methods for the Allied invasion of Europe in 1944.

Featured in this chapter is a collection of emblems manufactured by H.H.P. Whittemore & Co. of Attleboro, Massachusetts, one of the largest producers of military emblems during World War II. These small, hard enamel, gold plated screw back pins depicted Air Force units, Marine divisions and armored and all other divisions of the US Army.

Souvenir pins and medals are also displayed in this chapter. Souvenir pins from the military academies show a goat for the Navy and a mule for the Army. Other souvenir items would be pins depicting military bases, camps, forts or air fields throughout the United States. Souvenir medals include a sterling silver pin from the US Forces in England and a pin from the US Air Corps in England.

The additional variety of pins will excite collectors and enable them to pursue their own direction of collecting. The pins on this page represent paratroopers and airborne units. In addition, pins with four-leaf clovers made of sterling silver wish luck to the wearer. These pins can reach some lofty prices due to their rarity. Circa 1917 to 1945.

Each of these pins represent the U. S. Army. Note the two pins showing soldiers leaning against a heart inscribed "taken." The pin with a whistle attached to an eagle signifies the military police indicated by the crossed pistols. Circa 1917 - 1945.

U. S. Army pins with rifles attached most likely indicate Infantry service, which jokingly is referred to as "ground pounders" due to the amount of walking and marching the Army soldiers do. Older pins, such as the one with the canteen and the one with the hat suspended, and most of the small pins are from World War I. Most of the larger pins with large rifles are from World War II. Circa 1917 - 1945.

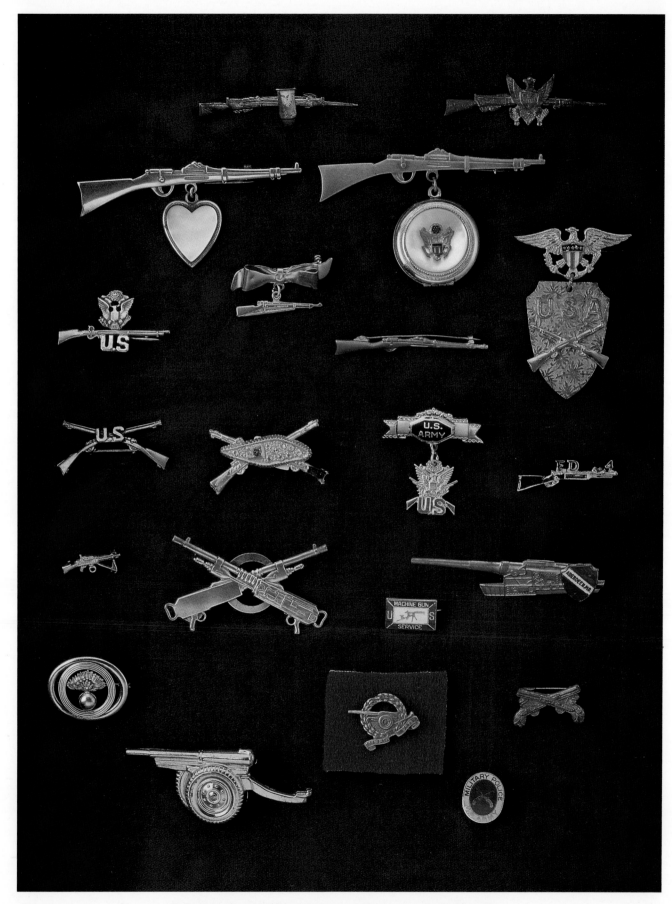

U. S. Army pins with rifles, cannons or machine guns can be found readily today. Pins with a bomb insignia indicate the Ordnance section and pins with large letters or numbers indicate the number of the army (such as the 5th Army). Circa 1917 - 1945.

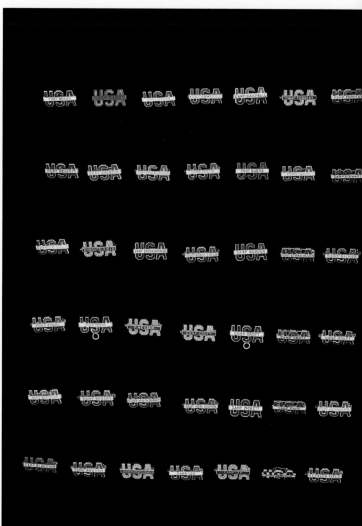

The U. S. Army pins here are mounted on a salesman's board and show that a pin could be ordered with any rank. The USA bar pins that indicate forts, camps and military installations should be exciting for collectors because they are not expensive (normally under $5). This group represents forty-two different pin types and thirty different locations. Circa 1942 - 1945.

A great variety of US Navy pins representing World War I and II.

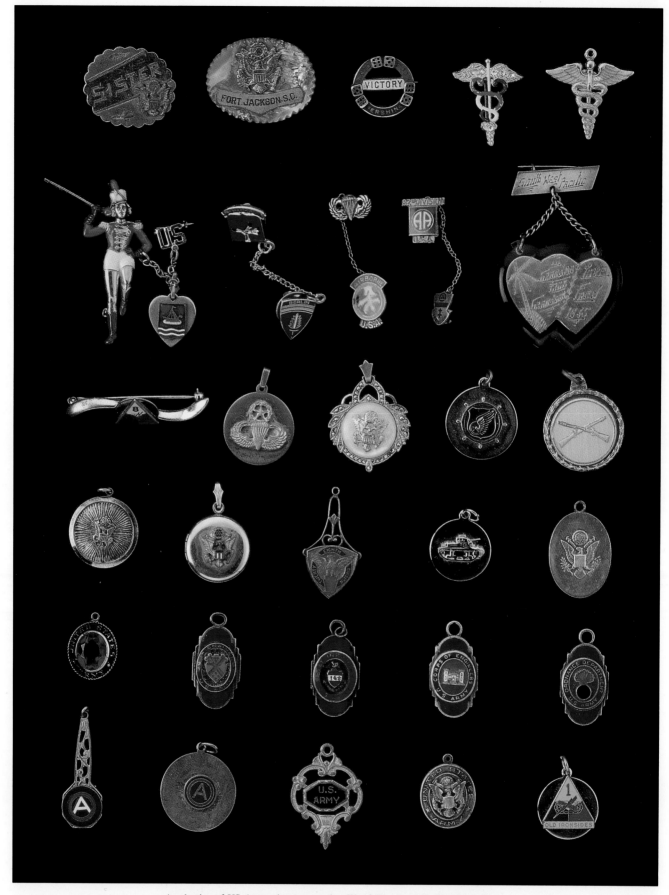

A selection of US Army pins representing World War I and II. The third pin in the top row is among the most valuable. It reads "Pershing" and "Victory" with three sets of dice. The enameled pendants have insignia of the Engineers', Ordnance, and Armored divisions. Circa 1917 - 1945.

The various Navy pins in this group are made with many types of materials, including sterling silver, gold, gold plate, plastics, wood, glass, potmetal and brass. The forms include ships, torpedoes, submarines, swords, spoons, sailors, bows, 4-leaf clover, and anchors galore. There is plenty of diversity for a collector. Circa 1917 - 1945.

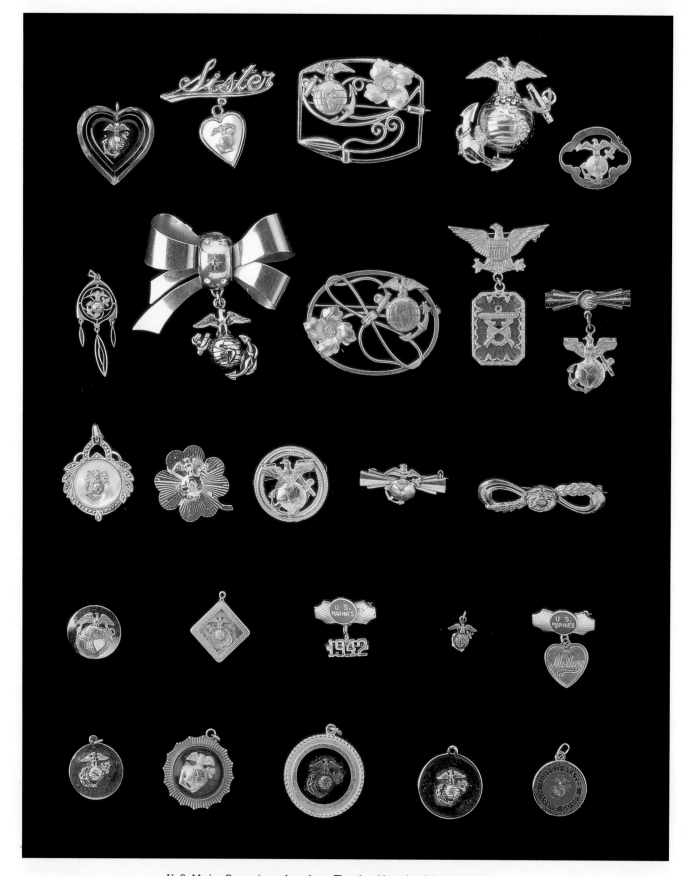

U. S. Marine Corps pins and pendants. The pin with eagle, globe and anchor at the top is the recognized symbol of the Marine Corps. This jewelry ranges from 1917 to the present. The earliest is the first pin in the second row (1917) and the latest are the last three in the bottom row (1960 to 1980). The middle pins in the first and second rows are among the most ornate to be found. Circa 1917 - 1980.

Army Air Force and U. S. Air Force pins and pendants found in their original box are very rare. The box on the left contains a matching miniature set of sterling silver wings and an 8th Air Force tie bar. The box on the right contains a rare mother-of-pearl set of wings. Circa 1917 - 1945.

U. S. Army pins on their original cards. Circa 1917 - 1945. Note the upper right corner is a pin of the 27th Division Army from World War I. Circa 1917 - 1945.

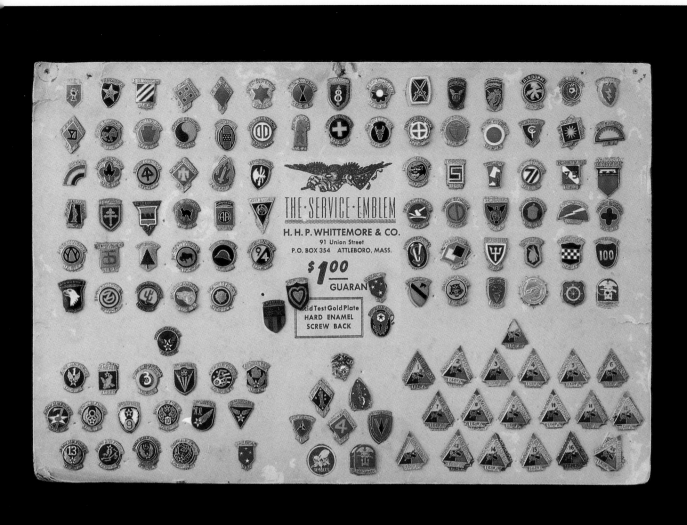

This large display card contains U. S. Army pins that originally sold for $1.00 each. The manufacturer, H. H. P. Whittemore and Co. of Attleboro, Massachusetts, was one of the largest producers of military items during World War II. Circa 1942 - 1945.

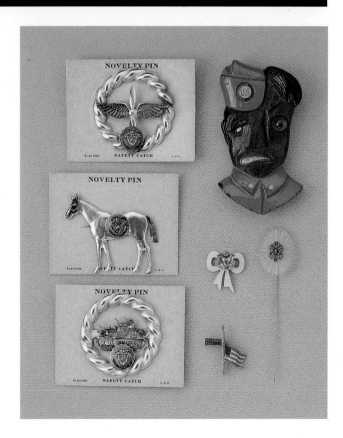

The tall stick pin shown at the right is from World War I. On the cards are rare World War II West Point pins made by Blecher. The carved soldier's head is a very rare pin. The right eye has a floating bead in it. The flag pin may be the only item from the VietNam conflict in this book. Circa 1917 - 1974.

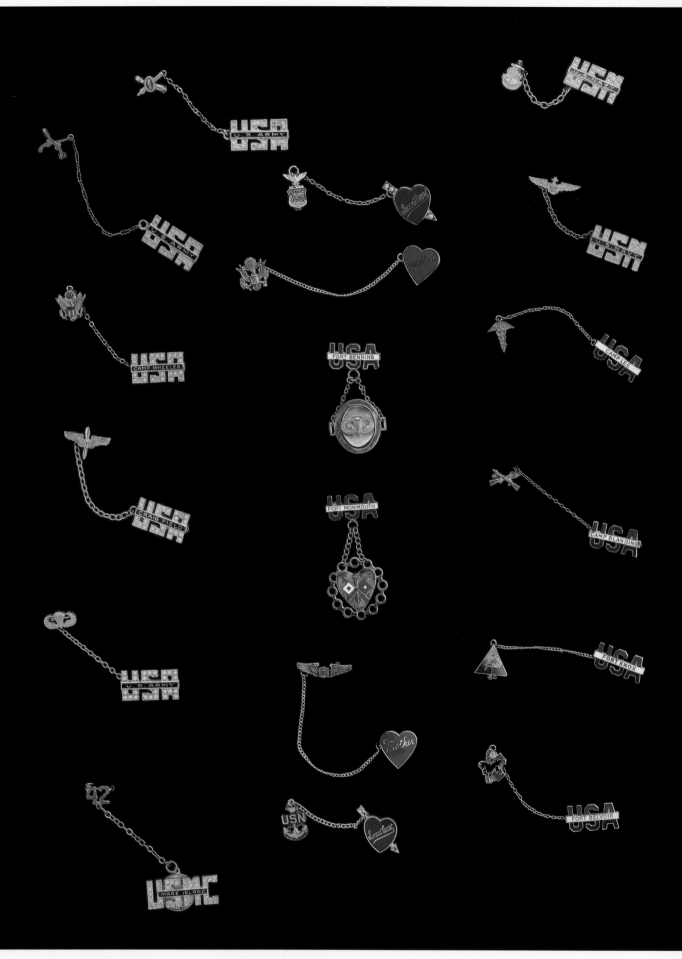

CHAIN PINS

Chain pins can denote patriotism, a branch of the service or an individual unit, or they can be a souvenir of a military base, fort or camp.

They were worn in both WW I and WW II and are still manufactured in modern day peace time. Manufacturers included Whittemorn & Company, Attleboro, Massachusetts; Uniscraft, J.O. Pollack, Chicago; Amico Company, Durocham, New York; and the Shiling Company, New York.

These attractive pins utilize many symbols in their design. In this collection there is an American flag attached to a fighter plane, and an Air Force Sergeants stripe attached to a USAF shield. Other attachments to pins include a tank, pistols, cannon, flags representing the Signal Corps, and the ranks of colonel, major, captain, lieutenants, corporal and sergeant. Collectors will also find attachments in the form of soldiers, the image of a bulldog, paratrooper wings and battleships attached to an anchor.

One of the most unusual chain pins is plastic. It has a WW II fighter plane attached by a chain to a pair of pilot wings. The unusual part is that the name "Kate" hangs from the chain.

In this collection of several hundred chain pins, only two have a locket feature as an attachment. This is a rare find.

Most chain pins are made of gold and silver metal alloys, sterling silver, 10k and 14k gold, brass, rhinestones, lead, enamel over metal, or copper. They could be purchased at the military exchanges or retail stores. Many U.S. companies gave them to their employees as a reward for their work effort.

Wives, sweethearts, and mothers of soldiers and sailors delighted in wearing attractive chain pins during the war years. Chain pins were a visible display of patriotism and in many cases love. Because of their attractiveness, availability and reasonable prices (in the $20 to $35 range), chain pins will always be a popular keepsake item.

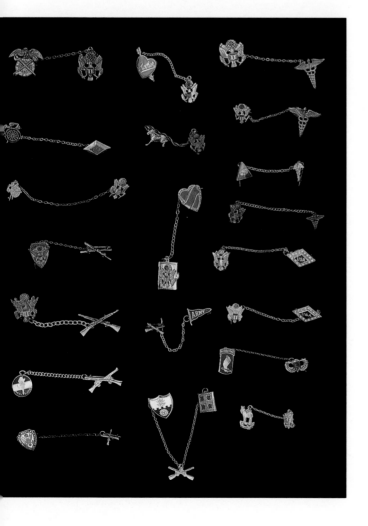

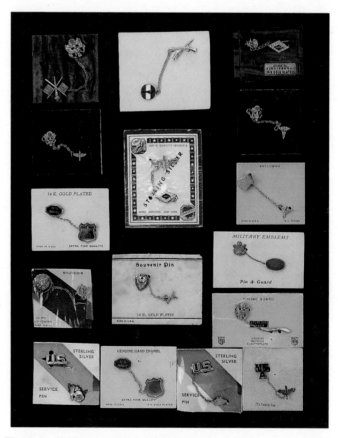

The chain pins shown on their original display cards sell at higher prices. In 1994, auction prices for some of these reached over $25. Circa 1942 - 1945.

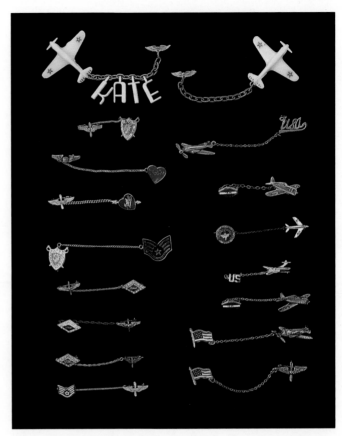

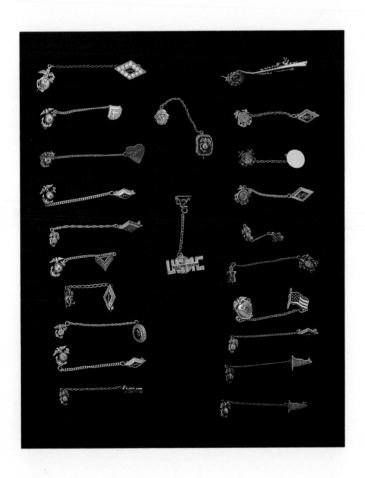

Chain pins, very popular during World War II, showed flags, planes, rifles, cannons, and tanks. Some indicated rank and the unit, and the attached heart might read "Mother," "Sweetheart," or "Wife." The group shown here include the Medical Corps, Army eagle, and the R.O.T.C. emblem. Circa 1940 - 1975.

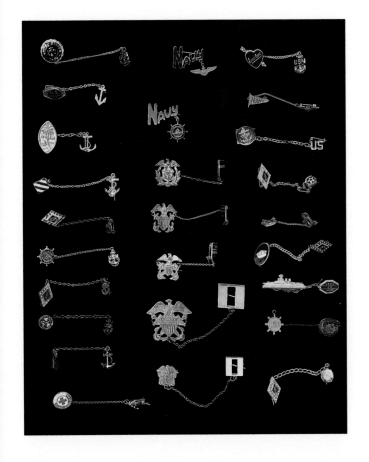

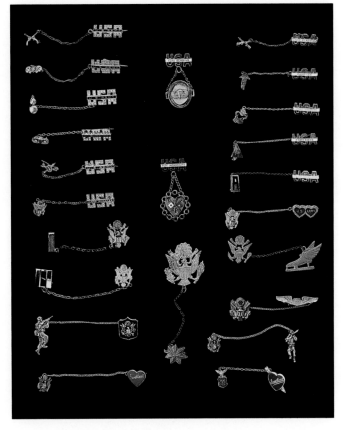

MILITARY HEADGEAR PINS AND LOCKETS

Military headgear pins and lockets were a great accessory that could turn an ordinary suit or coat into a patriotic statement. After all, what other sweetheart jewelry was in the shape of an officer's dress cap or helmet?

The pins pictured in this chapter show headgear attached to a rifle, a bugle, a single sabre, a sabre with a pair of gloves and a crossed sabre and rifle. One pin pictures a pair of riding boots attached to a soldiers hat.

Some of the headgear pins will open and there is a place for a picture. This locket feature will place this item in the $75 to $100 range. If not a locket type, a collector can find these pins in a wide range of prices from $15 to $100 depending upon age,

uniqueness, condition and the whims of the marketplace. Items found in their original box or on an original card will generally command more value.

Women delighted in buying and wearing this specialized area of sweetheart jewelry. A variety of materials were used in manufacturing these items including tin, plastic, lead, brass, jade, silver and gold metal alloys, mother-of-pearl and shells.

Most of the headgear jewelry in this collection represents the US Army. This is due, no doubt to the fact that the Army is the oldest and largest of the US Armed Forces.

Collectors will find a variety of colors in headgear jewelry including olive green, goldtone, red, white, blue, beige, brown, brass, silver and mother-of-pearl in a white and bluish tone.

This is a hard-to-find area unlike collecting full-size uniform headgear that is readily available, found in large numbers and designed to survive.

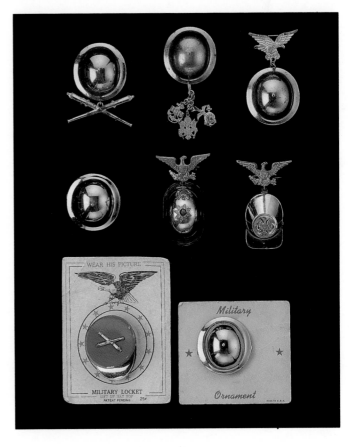

Military headgear and hat pins is an unusual area of specialized interest.
Shown here are brass hats as well as helmets. The hat pin at the lower right
corner of the top left photograph represents the crushed hat of General
MacArthur and is actually a locket. Circa 1917 - 1945.

PATRIOTIC PINS
"Let's Pull Together"

After months of disasters, the battlefield successes in the Pacific theater that began with Midway boosted morale on the home front, where American civilians by the millions were throwing themselves into the war effort. There was a drive to win--scrap drives, bond drives, and rationing all helped the American home front pull together.

Patriotic pins, pendants, buttons and medallions evolved naturally for a nation that wanted to visibly display its patriotism. These items were worn with pride on the lapels of coats, dresses, suits, blouses and sweaters.

The collectibles in this chapter depict subject matter that includes the American bald eagle, the American flag, a combination of American and Allied flags, Uncle Sam, soldiers, tanks, jeeps, oil and rubber conservation cut-outs, factory workers, shields, war heroes such as General Dwight D. Eisenhower and General Douglas MacArthur, and various novelty sayings, just to name a few. They were made of plastic, leather, wood, gold and silver metal alloys, tin, aluminum, mother-of-pearl, glass, ceramic and paper. Some items were handcrafted but most were manufactured.

Manufacturers included the J.M. Fisher Company, B.B. Company, Rochester, New York, the Packard-Murray Corporation, Prevue and Coro.

Many patriotic pins were manufactured very inexpensively and could be purchased for pennies. They were often given at bond rallies or patriotic rallies in defense plants.

Civilians working in defense plants would frequently be awarded production pins for outstanding effort on the job. This was similar to a uniformed soldier receiving a medal for exceptional effort. The most common production pin issued had an "E" in the center of a leaf circle and had red, white and blue flag banners on each end. On the back of this pin would appear the words "Army-Navy Production Award." These pins were issued attached to a card bearing the signature of the President of the United States. The card would read:

Message from the President of the United States

"An Army-Navy Production Award emblem is a symbol of service in the greatest production force in the world today--- a united and free army of American Workers."

Franklin D. Roosevelt

In a famous illustration by Norman Rockwell, Rosie the Riveter wears the Army-Navy Production Award with great pride. Rosie's contribution to the war effort was driving with a co-worker 3,345 rivets in six hours.

This chapter has its share of rare and unusual pieces including a World War I photo and identification locket on the original card. Both sides of the locket can be used for pictures. The card says "They all want your picture before you go to the front. Why not put it in this new attractive locket, or take one with you as a momento of your sweetheart or other beloved ones?"

Another rare collectible is the Liberty Loan Award made from a captured German cannon. This award is a medallion hanging from a red, white and blue ribbon. It was awarded by the U.S. Treasury Department for patriotic service on behalf of the Liberty Loans. It has a small button in the middle of the ribbon that says "Liberty Loan" and the letter "V."

Novelty items that are unique will always hold their value in the marketplace. A "Lets Pull Together" button pictured in this chapter features a moveable lever that allows Uncle Sam to hang Hitler over a tree limb.

Also of interest to collectors will be the small union production pin and the production and patriotic awards with company names on them such as the "Sperry " bracelet or the "Stearns & Foster" medallion that wishes an employee the best of luck and a safe return.

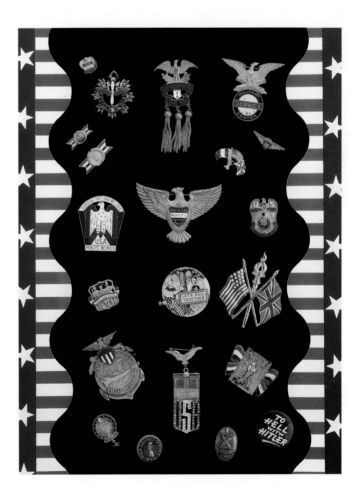

What are patriotic pins? They are drums, harmonicas, wooden soldiers, plastic sailors, ringing bells, carved soldiers smoking cigarettes, metal eagles of power, oil drums, rubber tires made from leather, wooden airplanes, and buttons commemorating war heroes. Circa 1917 - 1945.

These patriotic pins on their original display cards preserve a piece of history. Shown are plastic soldiers, efficiency pins, trumpets for sounding the call to victory, and Armistice Day pins. Circa 1917 - 1945.

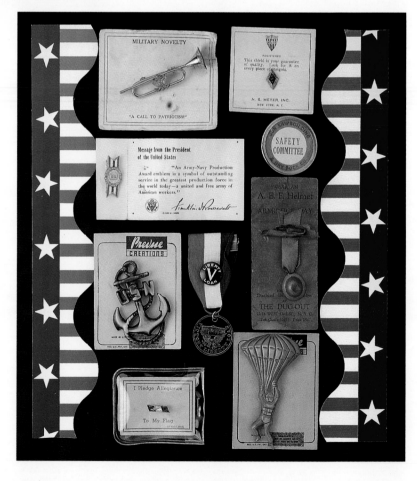

An endless variety of patriotic pins! Shown are flying flags, Adolf Hitler being hung by Uncle Sam, sailors on a string, the "E" Award pins for great efficiency and effort, three plastic soldiers marching, bracelets marked "A deFence Mfg. Co.", joined wooden hearts with Uncle Sam, "To Hell With Hitler" buttons, and medallions showing a good luck piece. Circa 1917 - 1945.

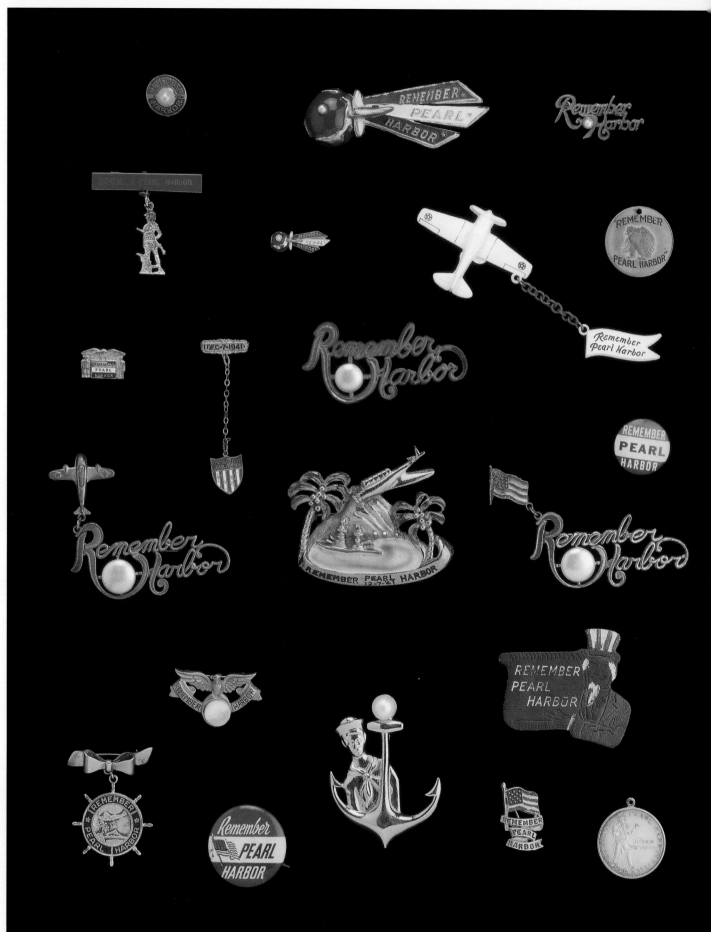

REMEMBER PEARL HARBOR

At 7:55 a.m. on December 7, 1941, the Sunday morning quiet of Oahu's Pearl Harbor was ripped apart when the first Japanese bomb dropped. Americans were stunned, outraged, saddened, and angered by the sneak attack on the key naval base for the United States Pacific Fleet.

The attack, which lasted about two hours, largely destroyed or put out of commission an entire battle fleet, destroyed Army and Navy aircraft on Oahu and resulted in the deaths of 2,403 American servicemen.

Only hours after the treacherous attack, President Franklin Delano Roosevelt declared war against Japan. "Remember Pearl Harbor" became the popular slogan that rallied the nation.

The United States reacted with all the strength and determination its people possessed. This inner strength was reflected in Pearl Harbor collectibles, one of the rarest and most specialized categories of military keepsakes.

Although there is a variety of articles emblazoned with the "Remember Pearl Harbor" motto, the fact remains there is very little for sale. Numerous articles were manufactured such as scarves, ties, song sheets, posters, postcards, cigars, stamps, war bonds, buttons, coins, chain pins, regular pins and lapel pins, necklaces and pendants. But there is not quantity in the marketplace. If you should discover a Pearl Harbor collectible, treasure it!

This chapter concentrates on jewelry that patriotic Americans wore after war was declared. It is necessary to note that Pearl Harbor was formed by two mouths of the narrow Pearl Stream. Its name came from the pearl oysters that once grew there. It is fitting therefore, that many pieces of "Remember Pearl Harbor" jewelry leave out the word "pearl" and have an inserted gem to represent the written word.

There are some styles of pins without a pearl however, and some simple red, white and blue pieces of costume jewelry with the famous motto.

In this collection there are articles made of tin, leather, sterling silver, metal alloys, plastic and resin. Most pieces are manufactured. Very few except for a leather Uncle Sam, are handcrafted.

Subject matter of Pearl Harbor jewelry includes Uncle Sam, Uncle Sam's hat, the American flag, the American eagle postured in a fighting position, the Liberty Bell, minutemen, sailors, anchors, miniature wings, fighter planes and a patriotic shield with the attack date attached.

The most common pin has "Remember Pearl Harbor" written in script. This chapter shows six different varieties of this pin. They were made in pewter, red and blue plastic, all white

plastic and gold and silver metal alloys. Most of these pins will have the distinguishing pearl and an attachment of a fighter plane or flag.

The rarest and most sought after Pearl Harbor collectible is the "Remember Pearl Harbor" pin that was sold by the Honolulu Community Chest. It measures two inches by two inches and features an island setting. It shows a Japanese fighter plane in a dive bomb position attacking a battleship. Large palm trees are on both sides. This pin can be found in two different styles. One shows a blue ocean on a gold background with green palm trees, the other style is all silver except for green palm trees. These pins have been observed at some collectible shows in the $150 range.

Pearl Harbor jewelry is associated with buying US savings bonds. Americans were encouraged to "wear your colors," buy bonds and "Remember Pearl Harbor," quite a large order for a single piece of jewelry.

Small lapel pins were also very popular. They are shown in this chapter in circular or diamond shape and also in the form of miniature wings.

Coveted patriotic collectibles are in this "Remember Pearl Harbor" group. The pins showing the island setting with a Japanese Zero Fighter may be among the most desired; two types are shown here and can range from $150 to $200. Circa 1942 - 1945.

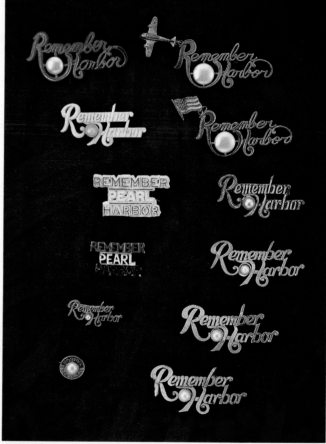

Some of the pins for Remember Pearl Harbor use a pearl in place of the word "Pearl." Few pins in this category ever come on the market and rarely will you find one on an original display card. Circa 1942 - 1945.

VICTORY PINS

V ··· —

Victory pins, distinguished by their "V" shape, were a special piece of jewelry in a special time. Never before had American people experienced such a nationwide sense of unity and commitment to a common cause -- the defeat of the axis powers. The nation's patriotic zeal was infectious and was expressed in many ways through "Victory"items such as pins, buttons, scarves, picture frames, postcards, trays, textiles, cookbooks, gardens, food and stationery just to name a few.

Victory pins were probably derived from the "Miss Victory" pins of World War I. These pins showed a woman in front of crossed flags that formed a "V." One is photographed in this section.

Often Victory pins will show Morse code in their overall design. The three dots and a dash, usually found at the base, spell out the letter "V." These Morse code symbols can be set in rhinestones or embossed in metal for a dimensional effect.

Collectors will be amazed by the variety of shapes, sizes, construction and subject matter of Victory pins. These pins can be octagon, circular, heart-shaped and free form. The letter "V" can be set in a ring, wings or earrings. In this collection there are pins incorporated into a red, white and blue ribbon, pins mounted on a locket and pins formed into novelties such as the hand and wrist.

The size of Victory pins in this collection range from one-half inch to almost four inches. Lapel pins in a simple form were quite small. Larger pins were suitable for a coat or breast pocket.

Manufacturers included A.E. Company, Utica, New York; Monet, Prevue, Fanfare, Accessocraft, Hayward, Kenneth Lane and Nema. Occasionally a handcrafted Victory pin will appear in the marketplace. In this section items of wood, crochet, beads and "Trench Art" bullets are shown.

In additional to commercial manufacturers, various companies and the US government would produce pins to be given away at fund drives. The telephone company distributed a pin "Serving for Victory."

Many Victory pins were so elaborate they had double attachments such as a "V" connected to another "V" by a chain. Other pins were made of coins and had the front and back of pennies stamped into their design. They usually had a hanger attachment.

Materials utilized in this collection include molded plastic, enamel over metal, resin, sterling silver, wood, bronze, rhinestones, handcrafted bullets, a symmetalic sterling and 14k gold combination, beads, and crochet, just to name a few.

Subject matter of Victory pins will feature the letter "V," the American eagle with its wings forming a "V," allied and American flags and branches of the service.

The Army is represented by an American eagle. The Navy shows an anchor with USN inscribed through it. The Marine Corps shows an eagle, globe and anchor. The Air Force is depicted by a set of wings and the Coast Guard shows a circle with a shield in the center and the words "The United States Coast Guard."

Of interest to collectors is the fact that Victory pins can show a connection with war production. One example is the pin with "Ships for Victory" slogan stamped on the front. Also, of special interest is the small In-service pin with a star centered in the letter "V." This is a very unusual piece of Victory jewelry.

In the marketplace, collectors will find V-J and V-E buttons which stand for "Victory in Japan" and "Victory in Europe." Other victory buttons will display patriotic pledges such as "I will do my best" or "I pledge to stay on the job." There are also buttons depicting slogans such as "Keep 'em flying," "Stars and Stripes Forever," "Be Alert," "Say it with Flyers," and "Liberty Loan."

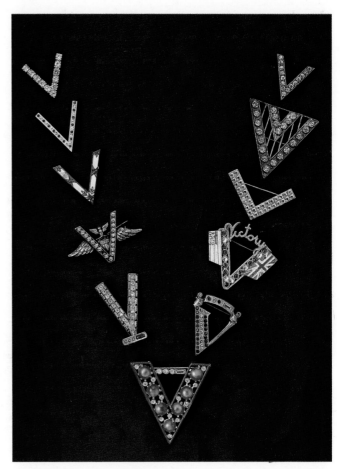

The use of rhinestones on Victory pins was common during 1943 to 1945. The military jewelry manufacturers joined the world of high fashion with amazing variety and attractiveness.

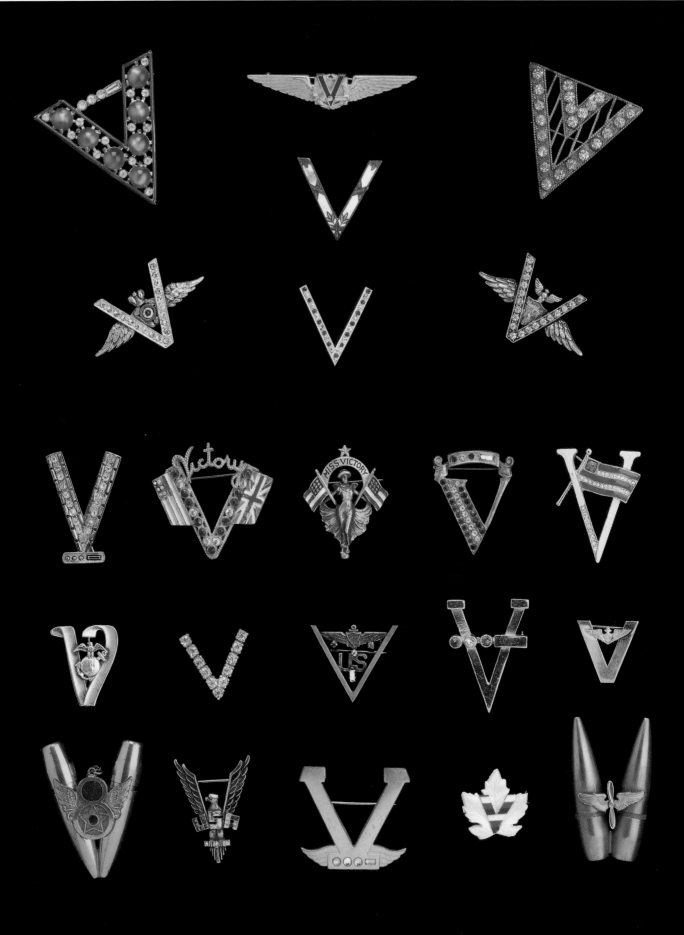

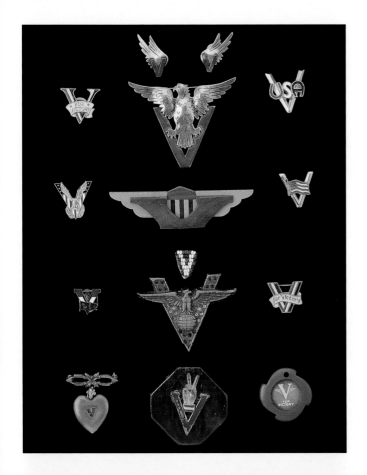
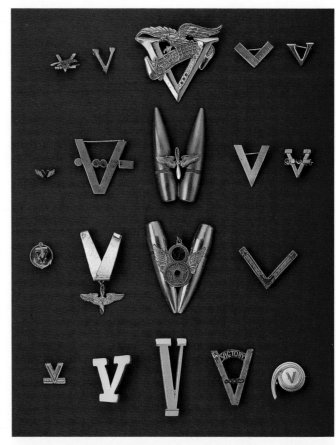
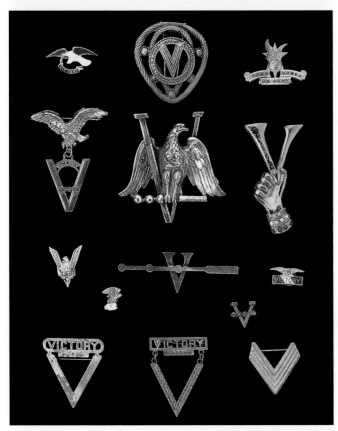

Victory pins range from huge "V" pins to very small pins with community service written on them. Shown are earrings and a matching eagle over a "V" pin, bullets cut in half and brazed together forming a "V," wooden "V" pins, and heart pins with a "V" in the center. Circa 1943 - 1945.

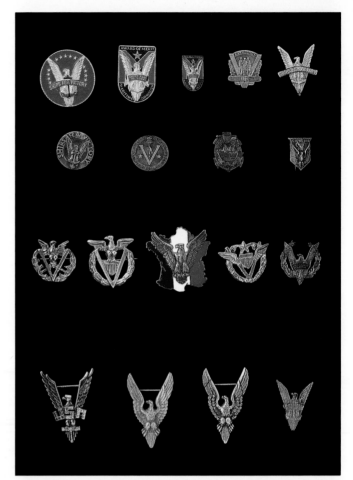

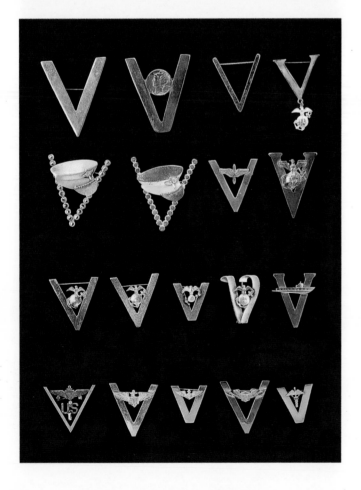

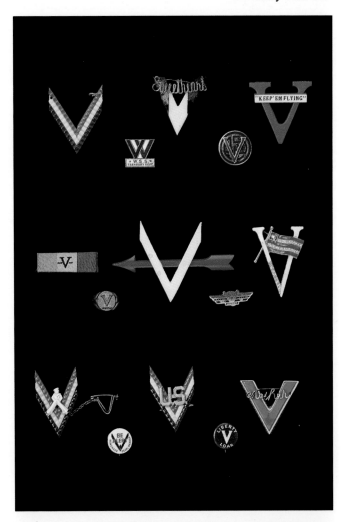

Shown are a variety of Victory pins with military emblems. Pictured here is an Army soldier's hat and a Marine Corps emblem on wings. There are buttons reading "V-J" for "Victory in Japan" and large and small V-pins joined by a chain. Pins with high pointed wings and pins with crossed swords form Vs. Some pins show three dots and a dash (Morse code V). Victory pins with wings or lightning striking were popular, and some have a place for a picture. Some are pennies with a V pounded into them or simple red, white and blue buttons that read "For Victory," circa 1943 - 1945.

The use of red, white and blue plastic was very popular. Victory pins on their original display cards are very rare. Circa 1943 - 1945.

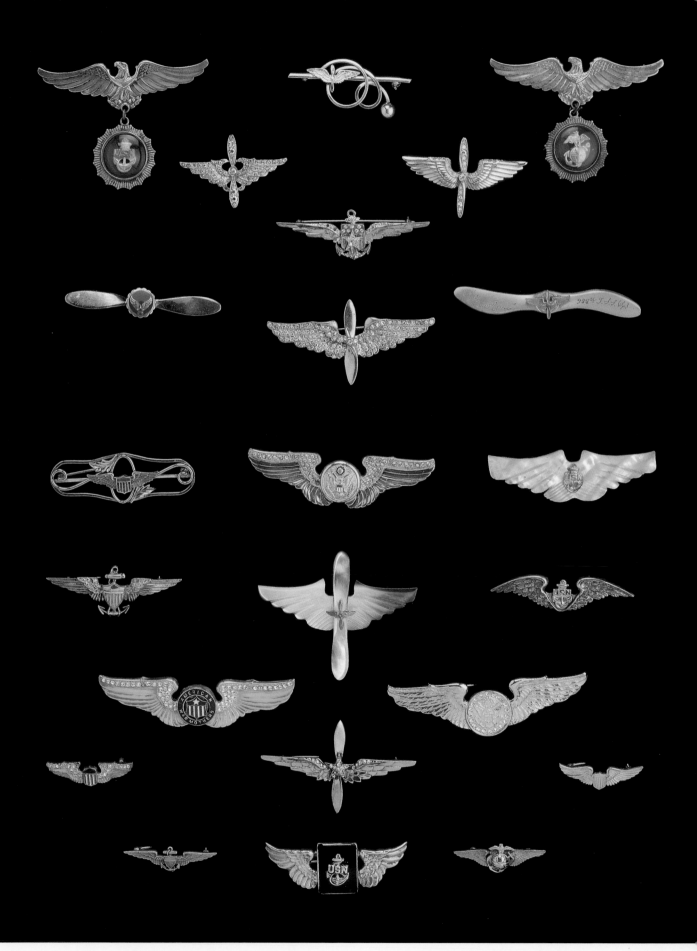

WINGS OF LOVE

"So fly with me, you mighty men,
With God's aid overhead,
We'll roar a million plane salute
In the land where the angels tread."
Lionel Croll

Off we go! Flying an airplane in the great World War was an exciting task. Loved ones delighted in wearing "wings" to display their pride in their aviator sweetheart or family member.

A large number of commercially produced wings were manufactured in 1942 to 1945. There were several hundred thousand wings produced in almost every conceivable medium. In this collection wings are represented in leather, Lucite, wood, a combination of Lucite and wood, mother-of-pearl, plastic, sterling, 10k and 14k gold and hard-cast metal.

Examples of wings that the collector will see in the market place include full-size, miniature, sweetheart and patriotic. Values can range from $2.00 to $175.00 depending on uniqueness and condition.

Some of the full-size wings were enhanced by rhinestones and black onyx by local craftsmen. The Lucite wings in this category are considered to be a part of "Pacific War Art."

Miniature wings were worn by loved ones on their lapel. Purchased for an average of about one dollar in the war years, today it is not uncommon to see them selling in the $25 to $35 dollar range.

Sweetheart wings came in a multitude of colors such as gold, brown, blue, green, white and bronze.

Patriotic wings were distinguished by a symbol such as a flag in the center. Many of these wings represented the 8th and 9th Air Force. The pictures and information given in this chapter clearly indicate the magnitude, vast beauty, and variety of collectibles that exist in this area.

Wings of the Marine Corps in large and miniature sizes are made from sterling silver. The pins with large silver wings carrying the U. S. Marine Corps emblem and the U. S. Coast Guard emblem in a plastic domed oval holder offer an unusual display. Circa 1940 - 1945.

Top to bottom: sterling silver Army wings with rhinestones, sterling silver Army paratrooper wings with red rhinestones, miniature U. S. Army sterling silver wings, and gold wash over sterling silver wings with rhinestones.

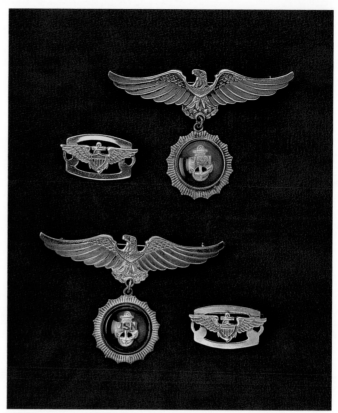

Four sterling silver U. S. Navy wings.

Top to bottom: Army goldtone wings, two Army sterling silver wings, and Army Lucite wings.

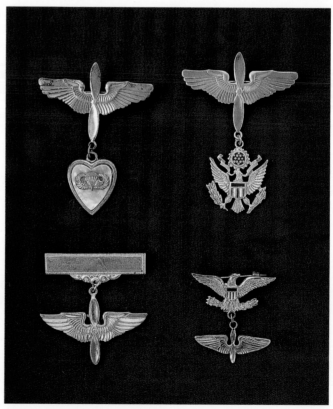

From top left clockwise, each made with sterling silver: Air Force wings, Army wings, and two Air Force wings.

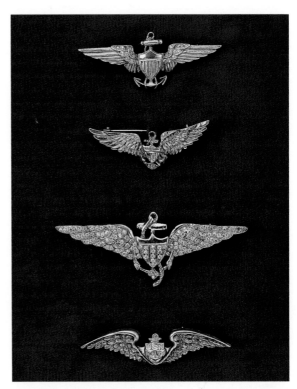

Four sterling silver U. S. Navy wings.

Top to bottom and rows left to right: Army gold washed metal wings, Air Force miniature sterling silver wings, sterling silver "AAF" with hanging wings, sterling silver Air Force wings with pendant, mother-of-pearl Air Force wings, sterling silver Ordnance wings, and sterling silver U. S. Army wings.

Four U. S. Navy wings in sterling silver and mother-of-pearl.

Five sterling silver U. S. Navy pilot's wings with shields.

U. S. Navy wings of sterling silver with a pendant watch and sterling silver U. S. Navy wings.

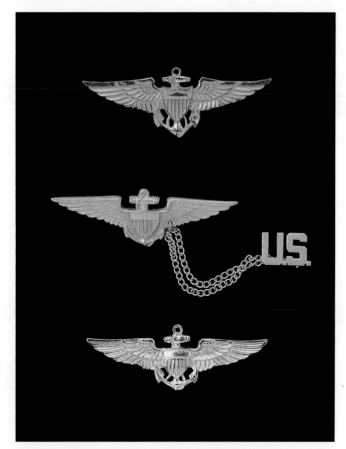

Three U. S. Navy wings in sterling silver and goldtone metal.

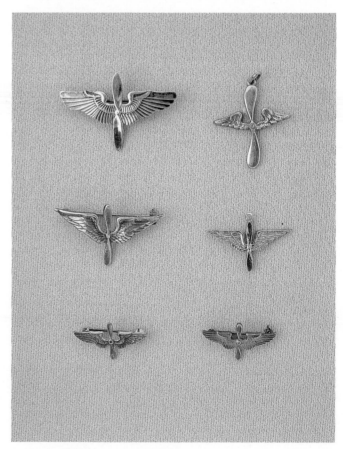

Six sterling silver U. S. Air Force wings.

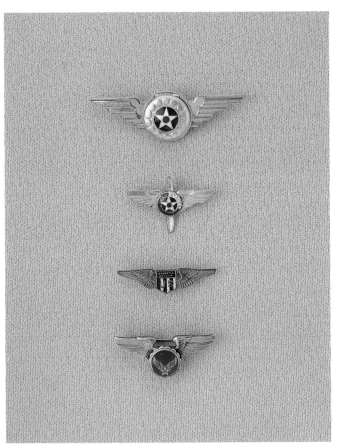

Top to bottom: U. S. Air Force wings of sterling silver with a locket, U. S. Air Force miniature wings of sterling silver, wings with a shield, and U. S. Air Force wings of sterling silver.

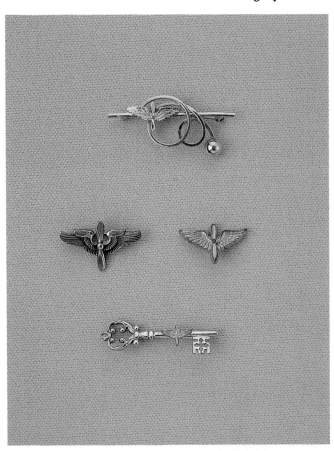

Four sterling silver U. S. Air Force wings, the top pin is a downed pilot pin which is very rare and valued at approximately $400.

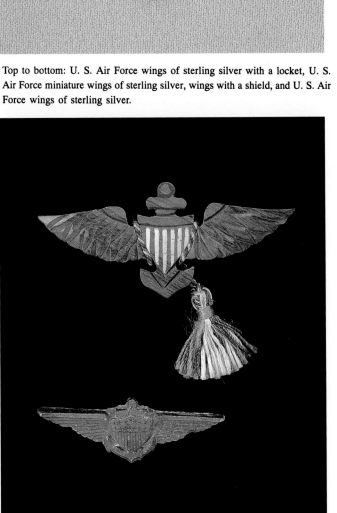

U. S. Navy wings made from leather (top) and resin (bottom).

Four sterling silver U. S. Air Force wings.

Six U. S. Air Force wings made from sterling silver.

Three U. S. Air Force wings handmade from Lucite. The second pin has wooden wings set on Lucite.

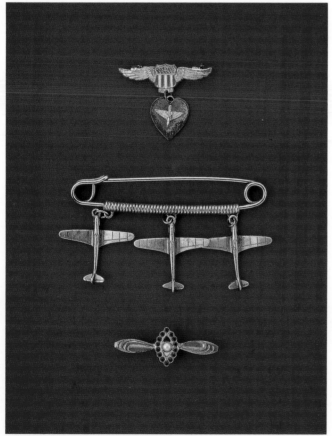

Top to bottom, all sterling silver wings: U. S. Air Force, a pin with three aircraft attached and a sweetheart wing pin with a pearl.

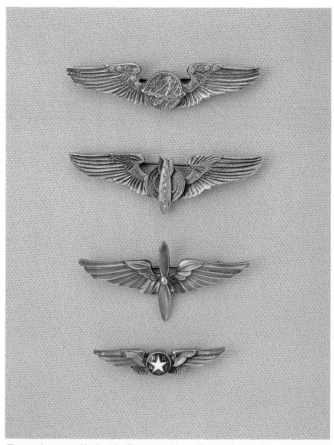

Top to bottom, U. S. Air Force sterling silver wings: the navigator, the bomber, not specific, and a miniature.

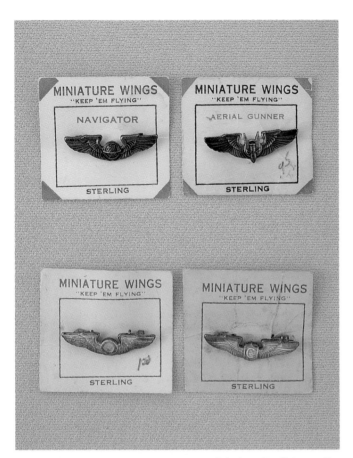

Four U. S. Air Force miniature wings on original cards, all in excellent condition.

Three U. S. Air Force wings made from wood, resin, and plastic.

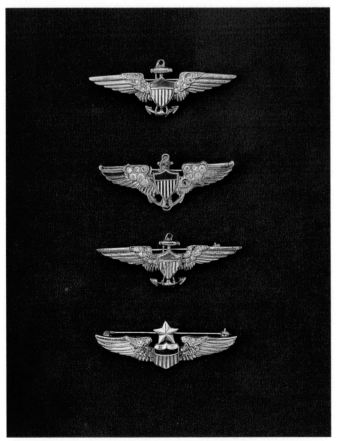

Four sterling silver U. S. Navy wings with rhinestones.

From top clockwise, four sterling silver U. S. Air Force wings: not specific, wing with a star, miniature with 22k goldtone, and a propeller pin.

SELECTED REFERENCES

Allmen, Diane. *The Official Identification and Price Guide to Postcards*. New York: House of Collectibles, 1990.

Cohen, Stan. *V for Victory, America's Home Front During World War II*. Missoula, Montana, Pictorial Histories Publishing Company, Inc., 1991.

Editors, TIME-LIFE BOOKS. *This Fabulous Century 1940-1950*. Alexandria, Virginia, Reprinted 1987.

Editors, *We Pulled Together And Won*. Greendale, Wisconsin, Reiman Publications, L.P., 1993.

Findley, Rowe. *1941: A World At War, World War II Remembered*. United States Postal Service, 1991.

Mueller, Laura M. *Collector's Encyclopedia of Compacts, Carryalls & Face Powder Boxes*. Paducah, Kentucky. Collector Books, 1994.

Parlett, David. *The Oxford Guide to Card Games*. Oxford, New York, Oxford University Press, 1990.

Rinker, Harry Jr., and Heistand, Robert. *World War II Collectibles*. Philadelphia, Pennsylvania. Courage Books, 1993.

Schiffer, Nancy S. *The Power of Jewelry*. Atglen, Pennsylvania. Schiffer Publishing Ltd., 1988.

Skipper, G.C., *World At War - Pearl Harbor*. Chicago, Illinois, Childrens Press, 1983.

Stein, R. Conrad. *World At War - The Home Front*. Chicago, Illinois, Childrens Press, 1986.

Tilley, Roger. *A History of Playing Cards*. New York, Clarkson N. Potter, Inc., 1973.

Warman's Americana & Collectibles, 6th Edition Radnor, Pennsylvania, Wallace-Homestead Book Co., 1993.

Williams, Vera S., W*ASPs - Women Airforce Service Pilots of World War II*. Osceola, Wisconsin, Motorbooks International, 1994.

CATALOGUES

"Sears Christmas Book," Chicago, Illinois, Sears Roebuck and Company, 1943.

MUSEUMS

Atlanta History Center, Atlanta, Georgia
Atlanta History Center Library and Archives, Atlanta, Georgia
The Jimmy Carter Museum, Atlanta, Georgia
The National Archives, Southeast Region

PERIODICALS

The American Legion Magazine. "The Home Front." December, 1992.

The Inside Collector. "The Home Front." June, 1994.

The National Geographic Magazine. "Insignia of the United States Armed Forces." "The Traditions and Glamour of Insignia." "Aircraft Insignia, Spirit of Youth."June, 1943, No. 6.

About the Author

This fascinating collection of antique military sweethea▮ jewelry and collectibles has been researched and assemble▮ through the enthusiastic efforts of Nicholas D. Snider.

Nick was raised in Cincinnati, Ohio, and was a commis▮ sioned Army officer serving in Georgia, Kentucky, and Germany After his service years, he transfered his military skills to th▮ United Parcel Service company where he began by driving a truc▮ in 1965. A number of years later, after moving through variou▮ district, regional and corporate levels, he found himself in th▮ technology end of the business. As project manager, he was re▮ sponsible for the development and deployment of the data co▮ lection device (DIAD), the electronic clipboard now used by 65,00▮ UPS drivers.

Presently he is charged with building an employee vo▮ unteer program world-wide for UPS, overseeing UPS volunteer▮ for the 1996 Olympics, and providing support from within h▮ corporation for former president Jimmy Carter's Atlanta Project▮

Nick is a true collector and his extensive travels hav▮ enabled him to collect not only distinctive military jewelry bu▮ also antique umbrella handles, Russian military items, Olympi▮ World Cup and Super Bowl pins, and classic cars for use in h▮ hometown parades.

Nick and his wife Betty and their three children, Chri▮ Tim and Susan reside in Atlanta, Georgia. Nick welcomes an▮ questions or comments at this address: Hotlanta, Inc., P.O. Bo▮ 501731, Atlanta, GA 31150.

VALUE GUIDE

Values vary greatly in the marketplace as a result of age, location, sellers knowledge or ignorance, condition of items, and the numbers produced. The prices shown here are merely a guide. Each buyer must make their own decision. A regret of not having bought an item can last a long time when so few items are available. All prices are in U.S. dollars($).

Page	Item	Value
p-6,7	Poster	75
p-10	Bracelet, 1-6	75-100
	Bracelet 7	100-125
	Bracelet 8-12	75-100
p-11	Bracelet/pendant	150-200
	On velvet card	100-130
p-12	Bracelet 1,3,6	100-125
	Bracelet 2,4,5	60-80
	Bracelet 7,8,9	30-50
p-13	Bracelet 1,2	30-50
	Bracelet 3	60-75
	Bracelet 4	75-100
	Bracelet 5,6	60-75
	Bracelet 7,8	50-65
	Bracelet 9, ivory	100-125
p-14	Top left, bracelet 1-5	65-75
	Bracelet 6-9	50-60
	Lower rt. pix 1-9	50-60
p-15	Bracelet 1	40-50
	Bracelet 2-6	60-75
	Bracelet 7	50-60
	Bracelet 8,9	65-75
p-16	Bracelet 1-7	75-100
	Bracelet 8	30-40
	Bracelet 9	75-100
p-17	Bracelet l, 14k	100-125
	Bracelet 2-9	75-100
p-18	Bracelet 1	35-50
	Bracelet 2,3	60-75
	Bracelet 4	75-100
	Bracelet 5	40-50
	Bracelet 6	100-125
	Bracelet 7,8,9	60-75
p-19	Boxed Bracelets	
	1,3,4,5,7	50-65
	Bracelet 2	60-75
	Bracelet 5	40-60
p-20	Bracelets 1-9	50-65
p-21	Top left, 1-9	50-65
	Lower rt. 1-9	50-65
p-22	Bracelet 1-2	75-100
	Bracelet 3	100-125
	Bracelet 4	75-100
	Bracelet 5	100-125
	Bracelet 6-11	65-75
p-23	Bracelet 1-5	75-100
	Bracelet 6-10	60-75
p-24	Bracelet 1-3	40-60
	Bracelet 4-7	65-80
	Bracelet 8	40-50
	Bracelet 9	75-85
p-25	Bracelet 1-10	65-80
p-26	Top left, 1-10	40-65
	Lower rt. 1	100-125
	Bracelet 2-5	40-65
	Bracelet 6,7	60-75
	Bracelet 8,9	75-100
p-27	Bracelet 1-4	50-65
	Bracelet 5	75-100
	Bracelet 6	100-125
	Bracelet 7-9	60-75
p-28	Bracelets, left side	
	Bracelet 1	125-150
	Bracelet 2	75-100
	Bracelet 3	100-125
	Bracelet 4	75-90
	Bracelet 5	150-200
	Right side, 1-8	60-75
p-29	Bracelet 1	75-100
	Bracelet 2	60-75
	Bracelet 3	70-85
	Bracelet 4,5	125-150
	Bracelet 6	250-300
p-30	Top left 1-8	60-75
	Lower right 1-7	60-75
	Bracelet 8	75-100
p-31	Bracelet 1	75
	Bracelet 2,3	60-75
	Bracelet 4,5	75-100
	Bracelet 6	125-150
	Bracelet 7,8,9	150-200
p-34	Compacts, top left	75-100
	Top right	100-125
	Center left	60-75
	Center right	60-75
	Lower left	60-75
	Lower right	60-75
p-35	Compacts	75-100
p-36	Compacts, top left	60-75
	Top right	75-100
	Center	60-75
	Lower left	75-100
	Lower right	60-75
p-37	Compacts	60-75
p-38	Compacts, except LR	75-100
	Lower right	125-150
p-39	Compacts, top row	75-100
	Center,	60-75
	Lower,	60-75
p-40	Compacts, top row	60-75
	Center left	75-100
	Center right	60-75
	Lower left	75-100
	Lower right	100-125
p-41	Compacts, top row	75-100
	Center	75-100
	Lower left, right	100-125
p-43	Compacts, top left	150-175
	Center left	100-125
	Top right	300-350
	Lower center	250-300
p-43	Compacts, top left	300-350
	Top right	60-75
	Lower left	100-125
	Center right	250-300
	Lower right	60-75
p-43	Compacts, top left	300-350
	Top right	60-75
	Lower left	100-125
	Lower right	60-75
	Center right	250-300
p-44	Mirrors, 1-6	20-30
p-45	Miniature Frames	
	Top left, row 1, #1	30-40
	Row 1, #2	60-75
	Row 1, #3	30-40
	Row 2, all	30-40
	Row 3, all	25-35
	Row 4	30-40
	Row 5, #l-2	15-25
	Row 5, #3	30-40
	Row 5, #4	25-35
	Row 6, #1	25-35
	Row 6, #2	15-20
	Row 6, #3	40-55
p-47	Handkerchiefs	40-50
p-48	All	8-12
p-49	Top left	12-15
Right		40-60
p-52	In-Service	
	Bracelet 1,2	75-100
	Bracelet 3	125-150
	Bracelet 4, (14k)	200-250
	Bracelet 5	125-150
	Bracelet 6	75-100
	pin	50-60
	pendant 1	75-100
	pendant 2	40-50
p-52	Lucite Hearts	30-40
	Eagle Pins	60-75
p-53	Necklaces/Pin	125-150
	All others	50-70
p-54	Top left	75-100
	Top center	50-65
	Top right	75-100
	All others	60-75
p-55	Row 1	30-45
	Row 2, #l	50-60
	Row 2, #2	30-40
	Row 2, #3	60-75
	Row 2, #4	25-35
	Row 3, #1	10-15
	Row 3, #2	35-50
	Row 3, #3	35-50
	Row 3, #4	25-30
	Row 4, #1	40-55
	Wing, #2	150-175
	Row 4, #3	20-30
	Row 5, #l,2	20-30
	Row 5, #3,4	40-50
	Row 5, #5	20-30
	Row 6, # 1,2	20-30
	Row 6, #3	40-50
	Row 6, #4	20-30
	Row 7, #1-7	20-30
	Row 8, #1	35-50
	Row 8, #2-4	10-15
	Row 8, #3	35-50
	Row 8, #5	35-50
p-56	Row 1, #1	35-50
	Row 1, #2	50-65
	Row 1, #3	35-50
	Row 2, #1,2,3	35-50
	Row 3, #1	60-75
	Row 3, #2	75-100
	Row 3, #3	60-75
	Row 4, #1	35-50
	Row 4, #2	60-75
	Row 4, #3	30-50
	Row 5,	
p-57	Row l, #1,3,5,6	35-50
	Row 1, # 2	20-30
	Row 1, #4	40-60
	Row 2, #1-3	15-25
	Row 2, #4, large V	60-75
	Row 3, #1-6	15-25
	Row 4, #1,2,3	25-35
	Row 5, #1,2,5,6,7	25-35
	Row 5, #3,4	50-65
	Row 6	40-60
	Row 7	75-100
p-58	Row 1	40-60
	Row 2	30-40
	Row 3	20-30
	Row 4	15-25
	Lower left, all	25-35
p-59	Top left	25
	Top right	50
	Center left	25-35
	Lower center	25-35
	Lower right picture, entire card	100
p-60	Pins, Rows 1,2,3	50-65
	Row 4, #1	10-15
	Row 4, #2,3	10-15
	Row 5, all	30-40
	Row 6, all	25-35
p-61	Row 1, #1	40-60
	Row 1, #2	150-175
	Row 1, #3	50-65
	Row 1, #4	25-35
	Row 1, #5	35-50
	Row 2	75-90
	Row 3, #l,2	40-50
	Row 3, #3-5	25-40
	Row 4, #1	40-50
	Row 4, #2	60-75
	Row 4, #3	30-45
	Row 5, USA gold	50-70
	Row 6, #1,2	25-35
	Row 6, #3	50-65
	Row 7, #1,3	25-35
	Right side, rings	
	#1-3	50-60
	#4	25-35
	#5	50-60
	#6	65-80
p-62	Center	50-65
	All others	60-75
p-63	Row 1, #1	75-100
	Row 1, #2	35-45
	Row 1, #3,4	45-55
	Row 2, #1	35-45
	Row 2, #2,3,4	45-55
	Row 3, #1,5	25-35
	Row 3, #2,3	30-40
	Row 3, #4	75-100
	Row 4, # 1,2,4	25-35
	Row 4, #3	40-55
p-66	British, Row 1, #1,3	50-65
	Row 1, #2	20-30
	Row 1, #4,5	30-40
	Row 2, #1,5	40-50
	Row 2, #2,4	30-40
	Row 3, #1,2	40-50
	Tie Pin, #3	50-70
	Ring, #3	75-100
	#4,5	40-50
	Row 4, #1-3	15-25
	Handpainted #4	50-65
	Row 4, #5	40-50
	Row 4, #6	25-30
	Row 5, #1-5	30-40
p-67	Bracelet #1,2	75-100
	Bracelet #3	40-50
	pins, Row 1, #1	30-40
	Row 1, #2	10-15
	Row 1, #3	75-100
	Row 2, #1,4	30-40
	Row 2, #2	40-55
	Row 2, #3	50-65
	Row 3, #1,3	20-30
	Row 3, #2	65-75
	Row 4, #1,3	25
	Row 4, #2,4	40-50
p-68	Top left, good luck	200
	Anchor	125
	Lower rt., Australian	40-60
p-69	Top left, lower left	40-60
	All others	75-100
	German, bullet pieces	40-60
	Bracelet	125-150
p-70	Row 1, #1,3	40-60
	Row 1, # 2	75-100
	Row 2, #1,2,3	75-100
	Row 3, # 1	75-100
	Row 3, #2	25-35
	Row 3, #3	50-65
	Row 4, #1	25-35
	Row 4, #2,3,4,5	60-75
	Row 5, #1	35-40
	Row 5, #2	25
	Row 5, #3,4	65-75
p-71	Row 1, #1,3,5	25
	Row 1, #2	40-60
	Row 1, #4	30-40
	Row 2, #1	35-50
	Row 2, #2	75-100
	Row 2, #3	40-60
	Row 2, #4	40-60
	Row 3, #1	40-60
	Row 3, #2	60-75
	Row 3, #3	30-40
	Bracelet #1	75-100
	Bracelet #2,3	50-65
	Bracelet #4	70-85
	In-service pins #1,2	25-30
	In-service pin #3	40
	Five leaves, #4	50-65
p.73	Lockets, lower left	50-60
	Lockets, lower right	60-75
p-74	Lower left	50-60
	Upper right	60-75
p-75	All	40-60
p-76	Upper left, coin type	100-125
	Lower rt., rifle	50-60
	Soldier, eagle	75-100
p-77	Lower left	40-60
	Upper right	50-75
p-78	Lower left, upper rt.	50-75
p-79	All	50-75
p-80	All	50-75
p-81	Row 1, #1	50-75
	Row 1, #2	100-125
	Row 1, #3	50-60
	Row 2, #1	50-65
	Row 2, #2	40-55
p-82	Row 1	50-65
	Row 2, #1	30-45
	Row 2, #2	60-75
	Row 3, #3	40-50
p-83	All	60-75
p-86	Pendants/necklaces	
	#1-5	50-75
	#6	40
	Center, Lucite	40-60
	Center, dog tag	50-60
	Black locket	200-250
	Right side, #1,2	50-75
	#3	25-35
	#4-6	60-75
p-87	Left side, #1	60-75
	Heart	60-75
	Book	50-60
	Square	60-75
	Center, #1	75-90
	#2	80-100
	#3	60-75
	#4	100
	Right side, #1,3,4	60-75
	Heart	40-50
p-88	Left side, #1	35-50

Page	Item	Value
	#2	40-55
	Heart	50-60
	#4	25-35
	USN	60-75
	#6	40-50
	Center	40-50
	Dog tag	40-50
	Right side, #1,3,6	35-50
	Heart	60-75
	Anchor	60-75
	Ship	25-30
p-89	Left side, #1-3	60-75
	#4	35-50
	Center, dog tag	35-50
	Wing/pearl	125-150
	2 round wings	40-50
	Sterling/glass	75-100
	Right side, #1,3	60-75
	#2	50
	#4	35-50
p-90	Lucite, all	40-65
p-91	Necklaces, #1	75-100
	#2	100-125
	#3	50-60
	#4, 6	125-150
	#5	60-75
p-94-95	Cards, all	1.00 each
p-96	A deck set	25-40
p-98-99	Postcards	3-10
p-100	Ration Books	
	Stamps, V-Mail	3-10
p-102-105	Patriotic envelopes	4-10
p-106	Pennants, Banners, Flags	
	WW I	50-65
p-107	WW I	50-65
p-108	Top left	50-65
	Lower left, right	25-35
p-109	All	25-35
p-110	Pillow covers	
	Top left	40-55
	Top right	40-50
	Lower left (WW I)	50-65
	Lower right	25-35
p-112	Top left, lower left	10-15
	Top right, lower right	
	Both WW I	40-50
p-113	Top left	25-35
	Top right	15-25
	Lower left	25-35
	Lower right	20-30
	Lower picture	
	Top left, lower right	15-25
	Top right, lower left	40-60
p-116	Pins, row 1, #1	40-60
	Row 1, #2	35-50
	Row 1, #3	55-75
	Row 1, #4	75-80
	Row 2, #1	30-40
	Row 2, #2	20-30
	Row 2, #3, 4	10-20
	Wings	30-40
	Eagle	15-20
	Row 3, #1	30-40
	Row 3, #2	50
	Row 3, #3(? pin)	70-85
	Spoon	30-45
	Row 4, #1, 3	25-35
	Row 4, #4	20
	Row 5, #1	30
	Row 5, #2	50
	Row 5, #3	40
	Row 5, #4	40-60
p-117	Row 1	40-50
	Row 2	35-45
	Row 3	40-60
	Row 4, #1,2,4	30-40
	Whistle, #3	60-70
p-118	Rifle pins	30-65
p-119	Row 1, #1,3,5	60-70
	Row 1, #2	70-80
	Row 1, #4	75-100
	Row 2	35-50
	Row 3	35-50
	Row 4,5,6	35-50
p-120	Gun pins	30-60
p-121	Pins	20-35
p-122	Rank pins, left	15-30
	right	4-5
p-123	Navy pins	

Page	Item	Value
	Row l, #1,3	40-60
	Row 1,#2	30-40
	Row 1, #4	60-75
	Row l, #5	25-35
	Row 2, #1,2 (WW I)	40-60
	Row 2, #3,4 (WW I)	70-85
	Ship, #5	40-50
	Row 3, #1	70-80
	Row 3, #2	95-110
	Row 3, #3,4	75-100
	Row 3, #5	25-35
	Row 4, #1,2	40-60
	Row 4, #3,4	30-50
	Row 4, #5	40
	Row 5, #1	25-30
	Row 5, #2	30-50
	Row 5, #3,5	30-40
	Row 5, #4	10-15
p-124	Row 1, #1	25
	Row 1, #2	30
	Row 1, #3	125-150
	Row 1, #4	30-40
	Row 1, #5	60-75
	Row 2, #1	35-45
	Row 2, #2,3,4	20-30
	Row 2, #5	40-50
	Row 3, #1	30-40
	Row 3, #2	15-25
	Row 3, #3	60-75
	Row 3, #4	15-25
	Row 3, #5	40-55
	Row 4, #1,2	40-50
	Row 4, #4	15-25
	Row 4, #5	30-35
	Row 5, #1	15-20
	Row 5, #2-5	35-45
	Row 6, #1	30-40
	Row 6, #2,5	15-25
	Row 6, #3	20-30
p-125	Top left picture	35-60
	Lower right	35-60
p-126	Pins/pendants	
	Row 1, #1	30-40
	Row 1, #2	55-65
	Row 1, #3	65-75
	Row 1, #4	60-70
	Row 1, #5	35-45
	Row 2, #1	100-150
	Row 2, #2	60-65
	Row 2, #3	75-85
	Row 2, #4	50-60
	Row 2, #5	40-50
	Row 3, #1	75-85
	Row 3, #2	100-120
	Row 3, #3	40-50
	Row 3, #4	30-40
	Row 3, #5	25-35
	Row 4, #1	25-35
	Row 4, #2	40-50
	Row 4, #3,5	15-25
	Row 4, #4	20-25
	Row 5, #1,4,5	15-25
	Row 5, #2	35-50
	Row 5, #3	20-30
p-127	Row 1	
	Box set	100-125
	Cloth bar	15-20
	Wings	15-20
	Box wings	40-60
	Row 2, #1	40-60
	Row 2, #2	25-30
	Row 2, #3 (14k)	75-85
	Row 2, #4	15-20
	Row 2, #5	20-30
	Rows 3,4,5	30-50
	Row 6, #1,2,3	30-45
	Row 6, #2,4,5,6,7	10-20
p-128	Row 1, #1	30-40
	Row 1, #2	35-50
	Row 1, #3,4	25-30
	Row 2,3,4	30-45
p-129	Card, single pins	7-10
	Lower right picture	
	Card pins	40-55
	Carved face	130-150
	Stick pin	45-60
	Small pins	15-25
p-130-133	Chain pins	15-35
p-134	Headgear pins and	

Page	Item	Value
	Lockets	
p-135	Lower left	35-60
	Lower right	50-75
p-136	Range	40-75
p-137	Patriotic Pins	
	Row 1, #1	15-25
	Row 1, #2	40-55
	Row 1, #3	50-65
	Row 1, #4	40-60
	Row 2, #1,2	15-20
	Row 2, #4	15-25
	Row 3, #1	25-40
	Row 3, #2	30-45
	Row 3, #3	25-35
	Row 4, #1	30-40
	Row 4, #2	65-80
	Row 4, #3	20-30
	Row 5, #1	50-60
	Row 5, #2	40-50
	Row 5, #3	35-40
	Row 6, #1	25-40
	Row 6, #2,4	20-30
	Row 6, #3	25-40
p-138	Lower left	20-45
	Upper right	30-50
	Eagle scale	125-150
p-139	Left picture	20-65
	Right picture, #1	15-25
	Row 1, #2	100-125
	Row 1, #3	40-60
	Row 2, #1	15-25
	Row 2, #2	50-60
	Row 2, #3	40-50
	Row 3, #1	15-25
	Row 3, #2	40-60
	Row 3, #3	25-35
	Row 4, #1	15-25
	Row 4, #2	25-30
	Row 4, #4	30-45
p-140	Range	40-65
p-141	Range	30-70
p-142	Pearl Harbor	
	Row 1, #1	25-35
	Row 1, #2	80-100
	Row 1, #3	30-45
	Row 2, #1,4	20-30
	Row 2, #2	50-75
	Row 2, #3	40-50
	Row 3, #1	25-35
	Row 3, #2	20-30
	Row 3, #3	40-50
	Row 3, #4	20-25
	Row 4, #1,3	45-60
	Row 4, #2	150-200
	Row 5, #1	25-35
	Row 5, #2	40-50
	Row 6, #1	35-50
	Row 6, #2	20-30
	Row 6, #3	40-50
	Row 6, #4	25-30
	Row 6, #5	35-45
p-144	Upper center	20-45
	Lower left	25-65
	Lower right	25-65
p-146	Victory Pins	
	Row 1, #1(red)	50-65
	Row 1, #2 (wing)	75-100
	Row 1, #3	40-50
	Row 1, #4	60-75
	Row 2, #1	40-55
	Row 2, #2,3	50-65
	Row 3, #1,2,4,5	50-65
	Row 3, #3	100-125
	Row 4, #1,4	40-50
	Row 4, #2,3	50-65
	Row 4, #5	30-40
	Row 5, #1,2,5	50-60
	Row 5, #3	35-45
	Row 5, #4	25-40
p-147	Upper left	
	Row 1, #1	25-35
	Row 1, #2(set)	100-125
	Row 1, #3 (USA)	25-30
	Row 2, #1	10-15
	Row 2, #2	40-60
	Row 2, #3	15-25
	Row 3, #1	20-30
	Row 3, #2	40-60
	Row 3, #3	25-35
	Row 4, #1	35-50

Page	Item	Value
	Row 4, #2	40-50
	Row 4, #3	15-25
	Lower left, Row l, #1	25-35
	Row 1, #2	35-50
	Row 1, #3	60-75
	Row 2, #1	45-60
	Row 2, #2	70-85
	Row 2, #3	35-40
	Row 3, #1	35-50
	Row 3, #2	20-30
	Row 3, #3	40-60
	Row 3, #4	15-25
	Row 3, #5	25-30
	Row 4, #1,2	25-35
	Row 4, #3	20-30
	Upper right, Row 1,#1	20-25
	Row 1, #2,5	15-25
	Row 1, #3	50-60
	Row 1, #4	40-50
	Row 2, #1	15-20
	Row 2, #2	35-45
	Row 2, #3	50-60
	Row 2, #4,5	20-30
	Row 3, #1	10-15
	Row 3, #2	35-50
	Row 3, #3	50-60
	Row 4, #4	35-45
	Row 4, #5	40-50
	Lower right, row 1, #1	25-30
	Row 1, #2	30-40
	Row 1, #3	15-20
	Row 1, #4	65-75
	Row 1, #5	25-35
	Row 2, #1,3,5	25-35
	Row 2, #2	30-40
	Row 2, #4	35-50
	Row 3, #1	15-25
	Row 3, #2	30-40
	Row 3, #3	70-75
	Row 3, #4	45-60
	Row 3, #5	30-35
	Row 4, #1	25-35
	Row 4, #3	15-25
	Row 4, #4,5	20-30
p-148	Upper left	
	Row 1, #1-5	40-60
	Row 2	30-50
	Row 3, #1	30-45
	Row 3, #2	60-75
	Row 3, #3	75-100
	Row 4, #1-4	35-50
	Lower left	45-60
	Upper right	30-50
	Lower right	
	Double V pins	75-100
	All others	25-40
p-149	Left side	25-50
	Upper right	25-50
	Lower right	
	Top two pins (same)	100-150
p-151	Wings, top left	50-65
	Top right,	50-65
	Lower left	35-45
	Lower center	60-75
p-152	Top left,	75-100
	Top right,	60-75
	Lower left	75-100
	Lower right	60-75
p-153	Wings, upper left	60-100
	upper right	75-100
	Lower right	75-100
p-154	Upper left, & right	60-100
	Lower left	60-100
	Lower right	40-75
p-155	Wings	
	Upper left	60-100
	Upper right, top pin	250-300
	Three others	35-50
	Lower left	40-55
	Lower right	75-100
p-156	Upper left	40-60
	Upper right	50-75
	Lower left	50-75
	Lower right	70-100
p-157	Wings, upper left	40-65
	Upper right	30-50
	Lower left	75-100
	Lower right	50-75